Series / Number 07-014

FACTOR ANALYSIS
Statistical Methods and Practical Issues

JAE-ON KIM
CHARLES W. MUELLER
University of Iowa

SAGE PUBLICATIONS
The International Professional Publishers
Newbury Park   London   New Delhi

For information address:

 SAGE Publications, Inc.
2455 Teller Road
Newbury Park, California 91320
E-mail: order@sagepub.com

SAGE Publications Ltd.
6 Bonhill Street
London EC2A 4PU
United Kingdom

SAGE Publications India Pvt. Ltd.
M-32 Market
Greater Kailash I
New Delhi 110 048 India

Printed in the United States of America

International Standard Book Number 0-8039-1166-1

Library of Congress Catalog Card No. L.C. 78-64332

96 97 98 99 00 01 02 28 27 26 25 24 23 22

When citing a professional paper, please use the proper form. Remember to cite the correct Sage University Paper series title and include the paper number. One of the two following formats can be adapted (depending on the style manual used):

(1) Iversen, G. R., & Norpoth, H. (1976). *Analysis of variance* (Sage University Paper series on Quantitative Applications in the Social Sciences, No. 07-001). Beverly Hills, CA: Sage.

OR

(2) Iversen, G. R., & Norpoth, H. 1976. *Analysis of variance.* Sage University Paper series on Quantitative Applications in the Social Sciences, series no. 07-001. Beverly Hills, CA: Sage.

CONTENTS

Editor's Introduction

FACTOR ANALYSIS: STATISTICAL METHODS AND PRAC-TICAL ISSUES extends the work of Jae-On Kim and Charles W. Mueller in their INTRODUCTION TO FACTOR ANALYSIS: WHAT IT IS AND HOW TO DO IT, also published in this series. The latter paper is a basic introduction to the technique of factor analysis; it focuses on the question, "Why do factor analysis?" and demands that the reader ask, "What assumptions are involved in using the technique?"

This paper takes the reader past the stage of reading books or articles which use the technique or of simply experimenting with factor analysis with one's own data. Here Kim and Mueller examine in greater detail, with more specific data analytic examples, the different types of factor analysis and the situations in which each is most useful. The distinction between confirmatory and exploratory factor analysis is discussed in greater depth than in the INTRODUCTION TO FACTOR ANALYSIS, as are the various criteria for factor rotation. Particularly useful is the discussion of the various forms of oblique rotation—and how to interpret the various coefficients from these analyses. Kim and Mueller also address the question of the number of factors to be extracted from exploratory factor analysis and discuss the methods of testing hypotheses in con-firmatory factory analysis. They also examine the problems involved in analyzing scale scores derived from these analyses. Again, a glossary is provided, as is a set of answers to questions frequently posed by users of the technique. The reader may well be disturbed by the answers to some of these questions—but paying them heed might save the analyst from making erroneous inferential leaps. The mathematics is largely self-contained, although there are some applications of matrix algebra in the text. The reader is advised to consult the introductory volume (07-013) when matrix applications are not readily understood.

Factor analysis has been used in economics to derive a set of uncor-related variables for further analysis when the use of highly intercorrelated variables may yield misleading results in regression analysis. Political scientists have compared the attributes of nations on a variety of political and socioeconomic variables in an attempt to determine what characteristics are most important in classifying nations (e.g., wealth and size);* sociologists have determined "friendship groups" by examining which people associate most frequently with each other (and not with other individuals). Psychologists and educators have used the technique to determine how people perceive different "stimuli" and categorize them into different response sets, e.g., different elements of language are interrelated.

As the authors indicate, these papers cannot possibly cover all of the aspects of factor analysis, since there are new developments in this area constantly emerging. However, if the reader can develop a more systematic knowledge of how the technique is to be used and what assumptions one is at least implicitly making, then these papers will have served their purpose well.

—E. M. Uslaner, Series Editor

*See Rudolph J. Rummel, *The Dimensions of Nations* (Beverly Hills, CA: Sage Publications, 1972).

FACTOR ANALYSIS
Statistical Methods and Practical Issues

JAE-ON KIM
CHARLES W. MUELLER
University of Iowa

I. INTRODUCTION

The conceptual foundation of factor analysis is simple and easy to learn. However, there are several reasons why mastering the method for practical application can be quite difficult. First, understanding the principles of statistical estimation in general requires more mathematical sophistication than is necessary for understanding the underlying conceptual model. Second, numerous methods of obtaining factor solutions have been suggested in the literature and even a relatively simple computer program is likely to provide many options at every stage of the analysis. Such complexities can be stupefying to the beginner and a source of uneasiness even to an expert. Third, the real research problem at hand is almost always more complex than the factor analysis model assumes to be true. For instance, (1) it may be that the level of measurement of some or all variables does not meet the measurement requirements of factor analysis, (2) some aspects of the model, such as independence of measurement error, may be unrealistic for one's data, or (3) one may have minor factors whose identification is not the primary concern but whose presence affects the identification of major common factors. The crux of the matter is that the researcher must in the end make some discretionary extrastatistical decisions. Fortunately, as will be shown, these difficulties can be overcome.

As we noted in the first volume, *Introduction to Factor Analysis: What It Is and How to Do It*, the researcher is more or less forced to rely

AUTHORS' NOTE: *We wish to express our appreciation and thanks to the numerous people who helped make the completion of this manuscript possible. In particular, computer assistance was provided by James Meeks-Johnson, Chia Hsing Lu, and Gayle Scriven. David Kenney, James Rabjohn, Elaine Black, and James Duane offered advice and suggestions on an earlier draft of the manuscript. A special thanks should go to Eric Uslaner, Lawrence Mayer, and an anonymous reviewer for their useful comments and advice.*

on existing computer programs for the actual solution, and these programs often provide standard default options that a user may depend on until some modification is felt to be necessary. Furthermore, as the researcher becomes acquainted with the variety of options in factor analysis, it will be evident that most variations are, to a large degree, superficial. In fact, there are several common threads underlying these variations. Even more important, the researcher will find that applying different methods and criteria to the same data will produce results that are equivalent for most practical purposes. In short, there is no need for the reader to learn and use all the options immediately. It is important, however, that the user *be aware of* the most important variations and options in obtaining factor analysis, and that this user appreciate right from the beginning the fact that there is no single definitive (or best) solution for most problems.

This volume assumes that the reader has a basic understanding of the conceptual foundation of factor analysis, such as that covered in the preceding volume. It is also expected that the reader is aware of the differences between the uncertainties inherent in inferring the underlying causal structure from an observed covariance structure (the logical problem), and the uncertainties inherent in making inferences about the population parameters from the examination of the sample statistics (statistical problem). Although these two problems are integrally intertwined in obtaining actual factor analysis solutions, it is important that the conceptual differences are kept clearly in mind. Before we discuss the statistical methods and practical issues, we believe it is useful to provide a brief recapitulation of the material covered in the first volume.

Review of Factor Analysis Basics

Factor analysis assumes that the observed variables are linear combinations of some underlying (hypothetical or unobservable) factors. Some of these factors are assumed to be common to two or more variables and some are assumed to be unique to each variable. The unique factors are then (at least in exploratory factory analysis) assumed to be orthogonal to each other. Hence, the unique factors do not contribute to the covariation between variables. In other words, only common factors (which are assumed much smaller in number than the number of observed variables) contribute to the covariation among the observed variables.

The linear system assumed in factor analysis is such that the user can identify the resulting covariance structure without error if the underlying factor loadings are known. However, ascertaining the underlying common factor structure from the observed covariance structure is always prob-

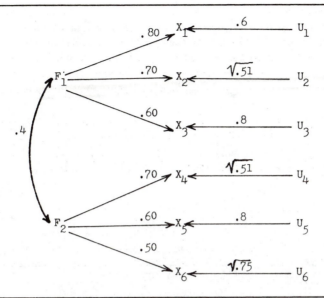

Figure 1: Path Model for Six-Variable, Two Oblique Factor Model Example, where the
observed variables represent opinions on:

X_1 = whether government should spend more money on schools,
X_2 = whether government should spend more money to reduce unemployment,
X_3 = whether government should control big business,
X_4 = whether government should expedite desegregation, through busing,
X_5 = whether government sees to it that minorities get their respective quota in jobs,
X_6 = whether government should expand the headstart program.

lematic. These basic uncertainties have nothing to do with statistical estimation and must be resolved on the basis of extra-statistical postulates—the postulate of factorial causation and the postulate of parsimony.

Given these postulates and the properties of linear systems, it is possible to identify exactly the underlying factor pattern from the examination of the resulting covariance structure, provided that the underlying pattern is relatively simple and that it satisfies the requirements of simple factor structure. For example, it was shown in the previous volume that the two-common factor model illustrated in Figure 1 can be recovered from the error-free correlation matrix shown in the lower triangle of Table 1. (In that volume, we noted that an initial maximum likelihood factoring solution, followed by oblique rotation based on Direct Oblimin, produced exactly the same factor loadings as shown in Figure 1. It was also noted that any computer program, whatever algorithm it may rely on, ought to reproduce such a pattern reasonably well.[1])

TABLE 1

Correlations for the Population (in the lower triangle) and for a
Simulated Sample of 100 Cases (in the upper triangle), Pertaining to
the Two-Common Factor Model Represented in Figure 1[a]

	X_1	X_2	X_3	X_4	X_5	X_6
X_1	--	.6008	.4984	.1920	.1959	.3466
X_2	.560	--	.4749	.2196	.1912	.2979
X_3	.480	.420	--	.2079	.2010	.2445
X_4	.224	.196	.168	--	.4334	.3197
X_5	.192	.168	.144	.420	--	.4207
X_6	.160	.140	.120	.350	.300	--

a. Reproduced from Tables 8 and 13 in University Paper 07-013.

In practice, however, the covariance matrix one actually examines is affected by a variety of random and non-random errors and will not be the same as the covariance matrix implied by the factor pattern in the population. For future reference, we have reproduced, in the upper triangle of Table 1, a correlation matrix which is based on a sample of one hundred cases from the theoretical universe defined by the factor pattern in Figure 1 (or by the covariance matrix shown in the lower triangle of Table 1). Note the discrepancies between the corresponding elements in the upper and lower triangles, and the fact that every sample correlation matrix from the same universe will be different to some extent from the population covariance matrix *and* any other sample matrix. Therefore, it is impossible in practice to recover the exact underlying factor pattern; one merely tries to find estimates of the underlying values which meet certain statistical and/or practical criteria.

There are three steps a researcher usually employs in obtaining solutions to exploratory factor analysis: (1) the preparation of an appropriate covariance matrix; (2) extraction of initial (orthogonal) factors; and (3) rotation to a terminal solution. Finally, we illustrated in the companion volume the ways in which these steps are handled by several computer packages and emphasized that it is relatively simple to obtain basic factor analysis information.

Basic Strategies and Methods to be Covered

The uses of factor analysis are mainly *exploratory* or *confirmatory* depending on the major objectives of the researcher. In both applications, the three basic steps—of preparing the relevant covariance matrix, extracting initial factors, and rotating to a terminal solution—are implicitly involved. Although theses steps may not always be followed in obtaining the final solution (especially in testing specific hypotheses), it is convenient to discuss major variations in factor analysis with reference to these steps. Hence, the first part of this volume is organized around these steps.

We have noted in the previous volume that there is a crucial option in choosing the basic input data—whether to use ordinary covariances (correlations) among the variables or to use similarity profiles among the entities. We have so far confined our discussion to the former and will do so here also.

In the initial factoring step, we have the *common factor* model, which has served as our model of reference, and *principal components* analysis, where the underlying rationale is different from "common" factor analysis, except that both methods are effective, and widely used, means of exploring the "interdependence" among the variables. The basic difference between the two approaches is that the principal components are certain mathematical functions of the observed variables while common factors are not expressible by the combination of the observed variables. An alternative in initial factoring is image factoring. Image analysis is different from common factor analysis in that the observed variables are considered a sample from the potentially infinite universe of variables, in which the image factors are defined as linear combinations of the variables. The similarities and differences in these approaches will receive elaboration in this volume. In addition, there are many ways of actually extracting the initial factors when the common factor model is applied. The extraction methods to be described in this volume are (1) the maximum likelihood solution (which includes canonical factoring of Rao), (2) the least squares solution (which includes Minres and principal axis factoring with iterated communalities), and (3) Alpha factoring. Alpha factoring can be viewed either as a variant of the common factor model or as an alternative strategy.

The rotation step involves two major options—the orthogonal rotation and the oblique rotation. The oblique rotation can be further subdivided into those which are based on the direct simplification of loadings in the factor pattern matrix or the indirect simplification of the loadings on reference axes. Within each of these options there are many variants. Most of these will be covered in the following sections.

Next, the question of how many factors to extract and retain will be discussed in a separate section. The main reason for including a separate section in addition to a section on methods of extraction is because of the need to introduce a few important "rules-of-thumb" which are found useful by many practitioners.

The section on confirmatory factor analysis is fairly elementary. We will introduce the reader to the notion of empirical confirmation of factor analysis models in general, and then provide illustrations of two simple but important uses of confirmatory factor analysis.

We will then discuss how to build factor scales in order to use them in other studies. We place this after the discussion of confirmatory factor analysis because some of the ways by which inadequacies in factor scale construction can be alleviated require the uses of confirmatory factor analysis.

In the final section, we cover a wide range of questions in a question and answer format. Most of the questions covered here are either not covered in the main text or are deemed important enough to deserve reiteration. Here we also offer some practical advice on issues for which there may not be consensus.

The glossary at the end of the volume is not intended to provide precise technical definitions of each term but, instead, is a convenient way of indicating in what context a term is used in this volume. Finally, the references in the volume are not meant to reflect the historical development or adequately give credit to the original innovations in the field. We have cited sources which we found to be valuable for our own understanding of the subject. The readers are advised to use these references in the same spirit, and we hope we do not offend scholars who have contributed to the development of factor analysis and have not been cited by us.

II. METHODS OF EXTRACTING INITIAL FACTORS

The main objective of the extraction step in exploratory factor analysis is to determine the minimum number of common factors that would satisfactorily produce the correlations among the observed variables. If there are no measurement and sampling errors and the assumption of factorial causation is appropriate for the data, there is an exact correspondence between the minimum number of common factors responsible for a given correlation matrix and the rank of the adjusted correlation matrix. (The adjustment of the correlation matrix requires inserting the communalities in the main diagonal.) That is, given no sampling error and an exact fit between the factorial model and the data, the communalities (actual values, not estimates) can be obtained, as well as the number of common factors, through the examination of the rank of the adjusted correlation matrix. In the presence of sampling errors, however, the rank-theorem cannot be relied on. The objective then becomes one of finding some criterion with which to evaluate the number of common factors in the presence of such sampling errors. As discussed in the preceding volume, the ultimate criterion for determining the minimum number of common factors is how well the assumed common factors can reproduce the observed correlations. Therefore, the objective may be restated as solving a statistical problem which involves finding criteria by which to decide *when to stop extracting common factors.* Following standard statistical logic, this involves determining when the discrepancy between the reproduced correlations and the observed correlations can be attributed to sampling variability.

We will begin by describing the basic strategy that is common to a number of extraction methods. It involves hypothesizing a minimum number of common factors necessary to reproduce the observed correlations. This means, in absence of any knowledge, starting with a one-common factor model. This "hypothesis" is evaluated by applying some criterion to determine whether the discrepancy between the assumed model and the data is trivial. If it is not, a model with one more common factor is estimated and the criterion is applied again. This is continued until the discrepancy is judged to be attributable to sampling error. (The reader should reflect back to Section II of the first volume where we assumed no sampling error, and the criterion was that the discrepancy be exactly zero.) It should be noted that actual computing algorithms may not exactly make such a sequential evaluation, but the principle of extracting the first k factors that account for most of the observed covariation remains valid.

Although in principle this basic strategy is straightforward, its application can take numerous forms because there are many criteria of maximum fit (or minimum discrepancy). Two major types of solutions that follow faithfully the common factor models we have described so far are (1) the maximum likelihood method (Lawley and Maxwell, 1971; Jöreskog, 1967; Jöreskog and Lawley, 1968) whose variants are canonical factoring (Rao, 1955) and procedures based on maximizing the determinants of a residual partial correlation matrix (see Browne, 1968), and (2) the least squares method, whose variants include principal axis factoring with iterated communalities (Thomson, 1934) and Minres (see Harman, 1976). In addition, there are three other major types of extraction methods: (1) Alpha factoring (Kaiser and Gaffrey, 1965), (2) Image analysis (Guttman, 1953; Harris, 1962), and (3) principal component analysis (Hotelling, 1933). The last method will be described first.

Principal Components, Eigenvalues and Vectors

We start with the discussion of principal components analysis for two reasons. First, it will serve as a base model with which the common factor model can be compared and contrasted. Second, it will provide the easiest means of introducing such esoteric concepts as characteristic roots (eigenvalues) and vectors, and their role in factor analytic algorithms. (We are not abandoning our goal of relying on mostly simple algebra, but certain familiarity with these terms is almost essential for a user of many computer programs. We urge you to try to follow our basic presentation.)

Principal components analysis is a method of transforming a given set of observed variables into another set of variables. The easiest way to illustrate its characteristics and underlying logic is to examine it within the bivariate context. Assume that there are two variables, X and Y, and also assume, for ease of presentation, that their distribution is bivariate normal.

A bivariate normal relationship with moderate positive association is depicted in Figure 2 by the use of contour maps. These maps show that because of the positive relationship between X and Y, the data points cluster such that higher values of X tend to be associated with higher values of Y (and vice versa), and therefore, more cases are piled up along the first and third quadrants than along the second and fourth. These contour maps form ellipses, the two axes of which are indicated by dotted lines. The principal axis (P_1) runs along the line on which the most data points are located; the second axis (P_2) runs along the line on which the fewest data points are located.

Now suppose that our task is to represent the relative position of each case in terms of only one dimension or axis. The logical choice for this reference axis is P_1 because in a sense this line is closest to the data points as a whole. The first principal component is then no more than a representation of cases along the principal axis. For one example, a case with a 1 on both X and Y will be represented by a larger value than 1 on P_1 and a smaller value on P_2. If we describe each case with respect to both P_1 and P_2 (in terms of points in a coordinate system), no information is lost and we can describe each case exactly regardless of the relationship between X and Y. However, we may say that the first axis (and the first component) is more informative in describing cases as the association between X and Y becomes stronger. In the extreme case where X and Y are linear functions of each other, the first principal component will contain all the information nɛcessary to describe each case. If X and Y are independent, there will be no principal axis and the use of principal components analysis will not provide any economy.

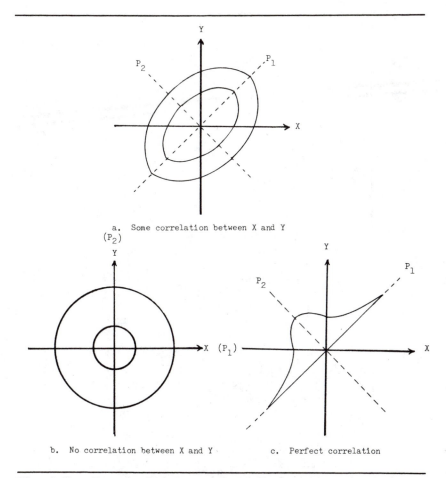

Figure 2: Some Examples of Principal Axes for Bivariate Distributions

Although we illustrated the principal axis in terms of an ellipse and a bivariate normal distribution, the concept of principal axes is not confined to relationships which are normal. In general, the principal axis is given by a line from which the sum of the squared distances from each point is a minimum value. A comparison with the least squares principle may help in explaining this. In finding a least squares regression line ($\dot{Y} = a + bX$) we minimize the sum of the squared distances between Y and $\dot{Y}$, i.e., we minimize $(Y - \hat{Y})$, where the distance is measured by a line parallel to the Y axis and perpendicular to the X axis. In finding a principal axis, we minimize the perpendicular distance between the data point and the axis (i.e., the distance is from the point perpendicular to the principal axis,

[16]

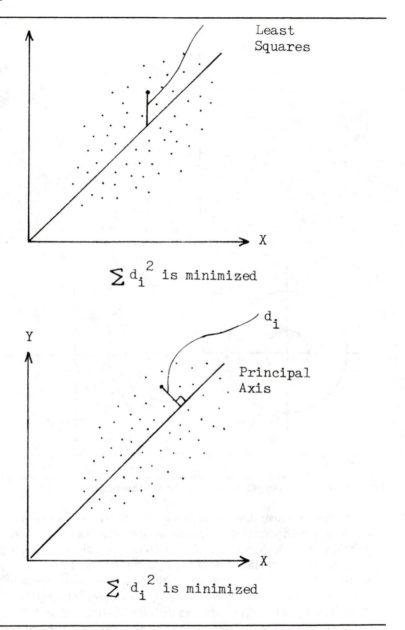

$\sum d_i^2$ is minimized

d_i

Principal Axis

$\sum d_i^2$ is minimized

Figure 3: Comparison Between Least Squares Regression Line and Principal Axis

not to X). This difference is illustrated in Figure 3. (See Malinvaud, 1970, for a discussion of least squares vs. orthogonal regressions.)

Once the first component is defined in such a way that the most information is contained in it (it explains the largest amount of variance in
the data), the second component is defined in a similar way with the condition that its axis is perpendicular to the first. In the bivariate case, therefore, once the first component is specified, the second component is known
automatically. Also keep in mind that unless Y is a linear function of X
and vice versa, there will be two principal components (we need two axes
to describe the joint distribution completely).

In deriving the principal components, we need not assume the existence
of hypothetical factors. The new axes are mathematical functions of the
observed variables. Even when principal components analysis is used as
a means of achieving economy of representation (this would be the case
of examining only the first few components), the objective is not to explain the correlations among variables, but to account for as much
variance as possible in the data. On the other hand, a factor analytic
decomposition would require only one factor (in this bivariate case), and
the primary aim would be to account for the *correlation* between the
variables. In sum, the former is oriented toward explaining variance, the
latter toward explaining covariance.

When there are more than two variables, the basis for defining the
principal components is the same. For example, for a trivariate normal
distribution, the three dimensional contours will resemble the shape of a
partially flattened football (an ellipsoid); the first principal axis is the line
running from one tip to the other, thus forming the longest line; the second
axis runs across the next longest distance, while being perpendicular to the
first axis (this is the part made wider by the flattening); the third axis
would be the shortest and would run along the part made less wide by
the flattening process.

The primary mathematical tool by which such hierarchical decompo-
sitions or transformations are arrived at is referred to as the characteristic
equation or eigenequation. Solving this equation produces eigenvalues
and eigenvectors associated with a matrix. The characteristic equation
(using matrix notation) has the following form:

$$RV = \lambda V \qquad [1]$$

where R is the matrix for which a solution is sought, V is the eigenvector to
be found, and λ is an eigenvalue. The solution is eventually based on a simpler
determinantal equation of the form:

$$\text{Det } (R - I\lambda) = 0, \text{ which translates into a bivariate matrix} \qquad [2]$$

[18]

$$\text{Det} \begin{pmatrix} 1-\lambda & r_{12} \\ r_{12} & 1-\lambda \end{pmatrix} = 0 \qquad [3]$$

which can be written out as

$$(1-\lambda)(1-\lambda) - r_{12}(r_{12}) = 0 \qquad [4]$$

(by definition of determinant),

$$= \lambda^2 - 2\lambda + (1 - r_{12}^2) = 0 \qquad [5]$$

(by expanding and grouping in a standard form).

The eigenvalues can now be obtained if you remember how to solve an equation $ax^2 + bx + c = 0$. At any rate the eigenvalues for a bivariate correlation matrix are:

$$\lambda_1 = 1 + r_{12}, \text{ and} \qquad [6]$$

$$\lambda_2 = 1 - r_{12}. \qquad [7]$$

Note that if the correlation between the two variables is perfect, one of the eigenvalues will be 2 and the other zero, and that if the correlation is zero, both eigenvalues will be 1.

Note also that the sum of the eigenvalues, $\lambda_1 + \lambda_2 = (1 + r_{12}) + (1 - r_{12}) = 2$, is equivalent to the number of variables and the product, $(\lambda_1)(\lambda_2) = (1 - r_{12}^2)$, is equivalent to the determinant of the correlation matrix. These properties hold for correlation matrices of any size. Most important, however, is the fact that the largest eigenvalue represents the amount of variance explained by the first principal axis, the second largest eigenvalue represents the amount of the variance explained by the second axis, and so on. Since the sum of all the eigenvalues is equal to the number of variables in the analysis (when the correlation matrix is used), by dividing the first eigenvalue by the m (the number of variables), we can also obtain the *proportion* of the variance explained by a given axis or component:

$$\begin{matrix} \text{proportion explained by} \\ \text{a given component} \end{matrix} = \begin{pmatrix} \text{corresponding} \\ \text{eigenvalue} \end{pmatrix} \Big/ m. \qquad [8]$$

The associated eigenvectors are found by imposing an arbitrary additional constraint that their lengths be 1. For this reason, the principal component loadings are obtained by multiplying eigenvectors by square roots of the respective eigenvalues, which correctly reflect the relative amount of variances explained by the corresponding data.

The simplest possible example is provided by the components analysis of the two variable (one-common factor) model of Tables 2 and 3 of the previous volume. The eigenvalues (arranged in descending order) are 1.48 and .52, which are equivalent to $(1 + r_{12})$ and $(1 - r_{12})$, respectively. The associated eigenvectors are, respectively, $(\sqrt{1/2}, \sqrt{1/2})$ and $(\sqrt{1/2}, -\sqrt{1/2})$. The "factor loadings" are given then by:

$$\begin{pmatrix} \sqrt{1/2} & \sqrt{1/2} \\ \sqrt{1/2} & -\sqrt{1/2} \end{pmatrix} \begin{pmatrix} 1/\sqrt{1.48} & 0 \\ 0 & 1/\sqrt{.52} \end{pmatrix} = \begin{pmatrix} .86 & .51 \\ .86 & -.51 \end{pmatrix}$$

The last matrix has the factor loadings that would be obtained if principal components analysis is specified in the computer program. Note that $\lambda_1 = (.86)^2 + (.86)^2$ and $\lambda_2 = (.51)^2 + (-.51)^2$.

To facilitate the forthcoming comparison of components analysis with common factor analysis, we will apply the former to the six variable correlation matrix of Table 1. We use error-free data in order to highlight its characteristics without fluctuations introduced by sampling. Table 2 shows the results of the components analysis. Three points should be noted: (1) there will be in general six components (although the last four will be minor and not reported here); (2) the first two components explain more variance than the first two common factors (61.6% vs. 41%); (3) the first two components do not completely account for the observed correlations, whereas the first two factors do (for example, $(b_{11}b_{21}) + (b_{12}b_{22}) = (.747)(.706) + (-.395)(-.409) = .6890$, which is much greater than the underlying correlation of .56).

Principal components analysis is similar to factor analysis in that both methods allow for data reduction. On the basis of the magnitude of eigenvalues, the researcher may have decided to use only the first two components. But to reiterate, it will not necessarily account for the observed correlations even though a two-common factor model can. There is another similarity between the two when they are considered as means of exploring interdependence of variables. Note the fact that if there is no correlation between any variables, there will be no principal component, because every component is as good or as bad as the other; each will account for only a unit variance. As the interrelations among the variables increases, the proportion explained by the first few components will increase.

One way to differentiate between the two is to say factor analysis represents the covariance structure in terms of a hypothetical causal model,

TABLE 2
The First Two Principal Components of the
Correlation Matrix in the Lower Triangle of Table 1

| Variables | Principal Components | | h^{2a} |
	F_1	F_2	
X_1	.749	-.395	.713
X_2	.706	-.405	.666
X_3	.651	-.417	.597
X_4	.595	.579	.623
X_5	.548	.529	.581
X_6	.488	.526	.514
Eigenvalues	2.372	1.323	Sum = 3.695
Percent of Variance Explained	39.5	22.1	
Cumulative Percent of Variance Explained	39.5	61.6	

a. These are not communality estimates in the strict sense of the term, because prineipal components analysis does not assume the existence of common factors.

whereas components analysis summarizes the data by means of a linear combination of the observed data. The choice between the two will depend on the researcher's overall objectives. The explanation of the correlation in terms of a smaller number of factors is achieved by an imposition of a hypothetical model. The mathematical representation of the linear combination of observed data does not require imposing what some may consider a questionable causal model, but it does not reveal any underlying causal structure, if such a structure exists.

The orientation of components analysis is, therefore, radically different from that of factor analysis. We wish to reiterate, however, why we have devoted considerable space to it. First, principal components analysis is often considered a variant of factor analysis. Second, principal axis factoring (to be described next) uses similar algorithms (eigen-equations), and the presentation of the factor method is easier with the knowledge of components analysis. Third, and most importantly, one statistic generated with components analysis still serves as the most widely used practical means of solving the number-of-factors question. (This refers to the criterion of "eigenvalue greater than 1," which will be taken up later.)

Variants in the Common Factor Model

Historically speaking, most of the earlier expository treatments of factor analysis identified the common factor model by a *principal axis factoring* procedure, which uses the decomposition strategies of principal components analysis as applied to the adjusted correlation matrix whose diagonal elements (of 1) are replaced by corresponding estimates of communalities.

Commonly used estimates of communalities are the squared multiple correlations of each variable with the remainder of the variables in the set or the highest absolute correlation in a row of a correlation matrix. After inserting these communality estimates in the main diagonal of the correlation matrix, factors are extracted in the manner of principal components analysis. That is, factor solutions are found by applying the same eigenvalue equation to the adjusted correlation matrix as was done in components analysis. (Hence, the name of principal axis factoring.) The equation solved in this case is:

$$\det(R_1 - \lambda I) = 0, \qquad [9]$$

where R_1 is the correlation matrix with communality estimates in the main diagonal. Although this method is still widely used, it is gradually being replaced by the least-squares approaches described below.

LEAST SQUARES APPROACH

The principle behind the least squares approach to common factor analysis is to minimize the residual correlation after extracting a given number of factors, and to assess the degree of fit between the reproduced correlations under the model and the observed correlations (the squared differences are examined). Because one can always reproduce the observed correlations by hypothesizing as many factors as variables, and because the fit will always increase as the hypothesized factors increase, the least squares solution assumes that we start with a hypothesis that k number of factors (k smaller than the number of variables) are responsible for the observed correlations.

The actual procedure for obtaining the solution is roughly as follows. First, assume that k factors can account for the observed correlations. (This step does not present any particular problem in practice because one can start with the hypothesis of one-common factor and increment the number of hypothesized factors until a satisfactory solution is found.) Second, obtain some initial estimates of communalities. (As indicated above, the squared multiple correlation between a variable and the remaining variables is used.) Third, obtain or extract k factors that can best reproduce the observed correlation matrix (according to the least squares principle). At this stage, the mathematical equation to be solved is exactly the same as equation 9 above. Fourth, in order to obtain the factor pattern that can best reproduce the observed correlation or covariance matrix, the communalities are reestimated on the basis of the factor pattern obtained in the previous stage. (The formulae for estimating communalities are given in equation 20 of Section II of the first volume.) Finally, the process is repeated until no improvement can be made. Hence, the name principal axis factoring with iterative estimation of communalities is derived.

The minimum residuals method or Minres (Harman, 1976) also is an iterative solution based on the same principle, but one which uses a somewhat different and more efficient algorithm. For this technique there is an approximate chi-square test which is appropriate for large sample sizes. Harman claims that this approximate test, which is independent of the particular method of factor extraction, can be applied to other methods of extraction, and can be used as a means for checking the completeness of factorization (Harman, 1975:184; for some reservations see McDonald, 1975). Although the test is appropriate when the sample is large, ironically, when the sample size is very large, minor deviations may be statistically significant. Therefore, Harman advises that one should not rely on the formal test alone but consider the number of factors obtained by such a test as only an indication of an upper limit, and try to retain only substantial and theoretically-interpretable factors (preferably after an examination of rotation results).

The application of principal axis factoring with iteration to the correlation matrix in Table 1 is presented in Table 3 below.

SOLUTIONS BASED ON THE
MAXIMUM LIKELIHOOD PROCEDURE

The overall objective of the maximum likelihood solution is the same as the least squares solution: to find the factor solution which would best fit the observed correlations. An informal description of the principle is as follows. We assume that the observed data comprise a sample from a population where a k-common factor model exactly applies, and where the distribution of variables (including the factors) is multivariate normal. What is assumed unknown, however, is the exact configuration of parameters, i.e., the exact loadings on each variable. The objective is then to find the underlying population parameters (under the given hypothesis) that would have the greatest likelihood of producing the observed correlation matrix. A somewhat different criterion based on the same principle involves finding the hypothetical configuration of factors in such a way

TABLE 3
Principal Axis Factoring with Iterated Communalities:
Political Opinion Example

Variables	F_1	F_2	h^2
X_1	.731	-.320	.637
X_2	.642	-.282	.492
X_3	.550	-.241	.360
X_4	.513	.473	.487
X_5	.441	.409	.362
X_6	.367	.340	.251
Eigenvalues	1.842	.746	
Percentage Explained	30.7	12.4	

that the canonical correlation between the k-common factors and the observed variables is the maximum. A third criterion ultimately leading to the same principle involves finding the factor configuration in such a way that the determinant of the residual correlation matrix is the maximum. All of these criteria are rather complex to apply in practice, and various versions based on the same principle vary considerably in the efficiency of the conversion process through the iteration. Jöreskog's (1967) solution is currently considered the best.

We will show in the following that in principle the procedure is not very different from other eigenequation solutions. The basic alogorithm can be expressed in the form of determinantal equations examined previously:

$$\det (R_2 - \lambda I) = 0, \tag{10}$$

where R_2 is given by

$$R_2 = U^{-1}(R - U^2)\, U^{-1} \tag{11}$$

$$= U^{-1}R_1 U^{-1}, \tag{12}$$

where U^2 is the estimate of unique variance at each stage. Equation 10 is different from equation 4 in that it uses the adjusted matrix R_2 in place of R and readjusts it in every iteration, and it is different from the least squares formulation in that R_2 is adjusted at every stage in such a way that greater weight is given to correlations involving less unique variance. Note that the part of equation 11—$(R - U^2)$—is the same as R_1 in equation 9; therefore, the only difference is the weighting factor in equations 11 or 12. In the maximum likelihood solutions, the unique variance is treated as "quasi" error variance, and therefore, the method assigns greater weight to the variables with greater communality (or less unique variance), and this follows the general principle of efficient statistical estimation in which less stable estimates are given less weight.

We mentioned earlier that the optimal procedure should be able to reproduce exact population values if the model is well-defined and data are error-free. Depending on the efficiency of convergence of a given program, some may not produce such a result; in principle, however, a good program should. In Table 4 we present the results of applying the maximum likelihood solution with the two factor hypothesis to the sample correlations presented in the upper triangle of Table 1.

As expected, the significance test indicates that the fit is adequate. The exact formula for calculating the χ^2-value is presented below merely to show that this value is dependent on the sample size, while the degrees

TABLE 4
Maximum Likelihood Two-Common Factor Solution Applied to
Data in the Upper Triangle of Table 1

Variables	Unrotated		Communality	Rotated Using Direct Oblimin Criterion	
	F_1	F_2		F_1	F_2
X_1	.747	-.300	.648	.817	-.027
X_2	.701	-.266	.562	.754	-.009
X_3	.599	-.176	.389	.602	.046
X_4	.428	.362	.314	.027	.547
X_5	.505	.605	.621	-.113	.833
X_6	.534	.248	.367	.202	.468
Sum of Squares[a]	2.132	.749		1.652	1.215
χ^2 with 4 degrees of freedom =	.825				

a. Sums of squares are equivalent to eigenvalues in the unrotated solution and this value divided by m gives the proportion of variance explained by that factor. In an obliquely rotated solution, they represent merely what might be called a "direct" contribution of each factor. The joint contribution (including that due to the correlation between the factors) is still equivalent to the sum of eigenvalues in the unrotated solution.

of freedom are independent of the sample size. The χ^2-statistic is given by:

$$U_k = N \left\{ \ln |C| - \ln |R| + \text{tr}(RC^{-1}) - n \right\} \qquad [13]$$

$\ln$ = natural logarithm, and tr = trace of a matrix
N = the sample size;
n = number of variables;
R = the covariance matrix;
$C = FF' + U^2$, where
F = Factor loadings and U^2, unique variance.

(In fact, the same formula is used in testing the least squares solution, the only difference being different estimations of F and U.) What is important is that for a fixed correlation matrix, the U_k value goes up directly proportional to N. The associated degrees of freedom are given by

$$df_k = 1/2[(n-k)^2 - (n+k)], \qquad [14]$$

where k is the number of hypothesized factors and n is the number of variables. Note that df_k is not affected by the sample size N.

The most important advantage of this method is that it provides a large sample significance test. If the χ^2 test indicates that the observed data deviate significantly from the k-common factor model, we would determine whether a k + 1 common factor model is appropriate. In an exploratory analysis, we would normally start with the hypothesis of one-common factor and proceed until the significance test indicates that a given factor model does not significantly deviate from the observed data. Although these sequential tests are not independent of each other, they may still be used without too much concern. (See Lawley and Maxwell, 1971.)

In practice, however, the difficulty with relying on the significance test alone is that we will end up with more common factors than are desirable if the sample size is large. Moreover, where the factor model is only an approximation to reality, a minor misfit between the model and the data can produce additional significant factors. Some related issues on how to determine the number of factors will be discussed once again in Section IV.

ALPHA FACTORING

In both least squares and maximum likelihood solutions, it is assumed that the variables one considers constitute the universe, and that the only sampling involved is the sampling of individuals. In Alpha factoring, however, *variables* included in the factor analysis are considered a sample from the universe of *variables*, while assuming that these variables are observed over a given *population* of individuals. Therefore, in Alpha factoring, the key emphasis is on psychometric inference, not on statistical inference in the usual sense.

Kaiser and Caffrey claim that this method is based on the principle that factor loadings are determined in such a way that the common factors so extracted have maximum correlations with corresponding common factors assumed to exist in the universe (1965:5).

Another way to think of this procedure is to consider the unique factors as if they are errors introduced by the psychometric sampling. Consequently, the communality estimates are treated as "reliabilities" in a measurement context. As a first step, the method produces a correlation matrix that is corrected for "attenuation":

$$R_3 = H^{-1}(R-U^2) H^{-1} \qquad [15]$$

where U^2 and H^2 are diagonal matrices of unique components and communalities, respectively. (H^{-1} is a diagonal matrix containing the reciprocals of the square roots of the communalities.) Then the determinantal equation associated with this "corrected" matrix is solved as usual:

$$\det (R_3 - \lambda I) = 0. \qquad [16]$$

Some comments on the similarities and differences between equation 16 and equation 10, and between equation 15 and equation 11, are instructive. The maximum likelihood solution scales the matrix by the unique variance while Alpha factoring scales it by the communality. Or differently stated, the former gives more weight to variables with greater communality, the latter does the reverse. As usual, the actual solution is complicated by the fact that one has to start with initial communalities and iterate these values for the final solution.

In Alpha factoring the number of factors to be retained is determined by the criterion that the associated eigenvalues should be greater than 1. This criterion is equivalent to the criterion that the associated generalizability coefficient, α (hence the name Alpha factoring) in the universe of variables, should be greater than zero. Here, of course, there is no significance test of the usual kind, because it is assumed that the population of individuals is considered.

The results from applying Alpha factoring to the sample correlation matrix reported in the upper triangle of Table 1 are presented in Table 5 along with results of image factoring, to be discussed next.

Image Analysis

Image analysis distinguishes between the common part of a variable and the unique part. The common part of a variable is defined as that part which is predictable by a linear combination of all the other variables in the set, and is called the *image* of the variable. The unique part is that part of the variable not predictable by the linear combination of other variables is called *anti-image*. In defining this decomposition, it is assumed that one is dealing with the universe of variables as well as the population of individuals; sampling of either kind is assumed not to be in operation.

Image analysis also assumes that this universe of variables is potentially infinite. For purposes of comparison we refer back to the two-common factor model specified in Figure 1. For that model the six variables specified constitute a universe in some sense. But in image analysis, the six

TABLE 5
Factor Loadings Based on Alpha and Image Factoring on
Error-Free Correlations Reported in Table 1[a]

| | Unrotated Factor Matrices | | | | | |
| | Alpha | | | Image | | |
Variables	F_1	F_2	Communality	F_1	F_2	Communality
X_1	.669	.437	.638	.575	.133	.348
X_2	.586	.384	.490	.538	.139	.309
X_3	.502	.329	.361	.477	.131	.245
X_4	.585	-.382	.489	.372	-.270	.211
X_5	.502	-.329	.360	.335	-.263	.182
X_6	.419	-.274	.251	.287	-.239	.140

a. Compare these values with those in Table 10, Kim-Mueller, University Paper 07-013, where the observed correlations were reproduced perfectly. In particular, note that the communality estimates by Alpha are very close to the true communalities whereas the communality estimates by Image factoring are relatively poor.

variables would be considered as a sample from an infinite universe of variables pertaining to the psychometric domain covered by the two-common factors.

If, however, we had all the variables in the potential universe for examination, the squared image of a variable would be equivalent to the *communality* of a variable defined in comon factor analysis, and the squared anti-image of a variable would be equivalent to the unique variance. (It is assumed here that we are dealing with standardized variables.) In other words, the squared multiple correlation between a variable and the remainder of the variables in this universe is the same as the communality of a given variable.

The images and anti-images defined for a sample of variables are called, respectively, partial images and partial anti-images. Although the partial images only approximate the total image, it is completely specified by the observed variables. In that sense, it is a radical departure from common factor analysis in which the common part of a variable is defined to be some linear combination of hypothetical factors, and never to be an exact function of observed variables themselves.

Given a sample of variables and their correlations, the image analysis constructs a partial image covariance matrix, which is given by

$$R_4 = (R-S^2) \, R^{-1} \, (R-S^2) \qquad [17]$$

where R is the correlation matrix and S^2 is the diagonal matrix whose elements are the variance of each variable unexplained by the other variables—or the anti-image variance. The process involved in equation 17 is, (1) to replace the main diagonal of R with the squared multiple correlation of each variable with the rest, and (2) to readjust the off-diagonal elements in order to make the resulting matrix Gramian. Then the eigenequation is applied to this matrix:

$$\det (R_4 - \lambda I) = 0. \qquad [18]$$

The number of factors to retain is, however, not given by the examination of eigenvalues for equation 18 but by the eigenvalues greater than 1 from the equation in which a different matrix $(S^{-1}RS^{-1})$ is put in the place of R_4. Usually, the number of factors so retained is relatively large—approaching one-half of the variables in the analysis. Kaiser suggests that insignificant and uninterpretable factors be dropped after proper rotations. Some statistics generated by image factoring on the sample correlation matrix are presented in Table 5 along with other results.

III. METHODS OF ROTATION

The initial factoring step usually determines the minimum *number* of factors that can adequately account for observed correlations, and in the process determines the communalities of each variable. The next step in factor analysis involves finding simpler and more easily interpretable factors through rotations, while keeping the number of factors and communalities of each variable fixed.

All the solutions examined in the previous section produce initial factors that are orthogonal and that are arranged in a descending order of importance. These two properties of the factor solution are not inherent in the data structure; they are arbitrary impositions placed on data to make the solutions unique and definable in some sense. The consequences of making these arbitrary impositions are that (1) the factorial complexity of variables is likely to be greater than one, regardless of the underlying true model—that is, variables will have substantial loadings on more than one factor; (2) except for the first factor, the remaining factors are bipolar—that is, some variables have positive loadings on a factor while others have negative loadings. (If these descriptions do not seem meaningful, refer to Section II of the preceding volume and examine some of the factor patterns.)

There are basically three different approaches to the rotation problem. The first approach is to examine the pattern of variables graphically as we did in Section II of the previous volume, and then rotate the axis or define new axes in such a way that the new axes best satisfy one's criterion of simple and meaningful structure. When there are clear clusters of variables, well separated from each other (as in Figure 17 of the previous volume), the simple structure would be achieved if each axis is made to run through a cluster. But whenever the pattern is not very clear or there are many factors to examine, such a graphical rotation is not practical for a novice.

The second approach is to rely on some analytic rotation method that is free of subjective judgment, at least after a particular criterion of simplicity is chosen. There are two different subtypes in this approach—one is the method of orthogonal rotation and the other is oblique rotation. Within each subtype there are numerous variations, but only a few well known and widely used versions will be described in this section.

The third approach to rotation is to define a target matrix or configuration before actual rotation. The objective of such rotation is to find the factor patterns that are closest to the given target matrix. Since the specification of target matrix presumes certain knowledge or a hypothesis about the nature of the factor structure, this strategy approaches confirmatory factor analysis.

Graphic Rotation, Simple Structure, and Reference Axes

The graphic rotation procedure is difficult to apply whenever the clustering is not clear or there are more than two factors to examine. We will touch on this subject merely to set the stage for the analytic rotations. (Readers may consult Mulaik (1972) for a good introduction to graphic rotation.)

The manifest goal of all the rotations is to achieve the simplest possible factor structure. Unfortunately, the concept of simplicity itself is not so straightforward as to allow for a formal and undisputed criterion. The most ambitious attempt to define a simple structure is made by Thurstone (1947), but it is generally conceded today that not all of his criteria are definable in analytic terms. Since an understanding of Thurstone's criteria requires knowledge of hyperplanes or subspaces, we merely present Mulaik's (1972:220) excellent account of these criteria for those who have some knowledge of vector spaces. (In Mulaik's description, r refers to the number of common factors, and V is the reference structure matrix consisting of a reference axis.)

(1) Each row of the reference-structure matrix V should have at least one zero. This is the basic assumption of simple structure as implied in the definition of simple structure given at the onset of this section.

(2) For each column k of the reference-structure matrix V there should be a set of at least r linearly independent observed variables whose correlations (as found in the kth column of V) with the kth reference-axis variable are zero. This criterion is needed to overdetermine the corresponding reference axis.

(3) For every pair of columns of V there should be several zero entries in one column corresponding to nonzero entries in the other. This requirement assures the distinctness of the reference axes and their corresponding subspaces of $r -1$ dimensions of the common-factor space.

(4) When four or more common factors are obtained, each pair of columns of V should have a proportion of corresponding zero entries. This requirement assures that each reference axis is pertinent to only a few of the observed variables and thus guarantees a separation of the observed variables into distinct clusters.

(5) For every pair of columns of V there should be only a small number of corresponding entries in both columns which do not vanish. This criterion further ensures the simplicity of the variables.

These criteria are ultimately based on two somewhat different considerations: (1) the need to define criteria of a simple factor structure, and (2) the need to specify conditions under which a simple structure is unambiguously identified. What makes Thurstone's criteria difficult for novices to understand is the technical and complex literature directed toward the second consideration. For our purposes, however, the first consideration is primary while the second one represents technical requirements which we would rather leave for the specialists to worry about.

Although it is difficult to specify what constitutes a minimum requirement for "simple structure," it is rather easy to specify what constitutes the simplest possible structure, given r number of factors and n variables. The factor structure is the simplest if all the variables have factorial complexity of one—i.e., each variable has nonzero loadings on only one common factor. Given two or more common factors, this means that in the simplest pattern matrix (1) each row will have only one nonzero element, (2) each column will contain some zeros, and (3) between any pair of columns, the nonzero elements do not overlap.

With real data, one is not likely to see such a simple structure. So the task becomes how to "define" factor structures that are "closest" to the simplest structure. Here, specialists diverge in their definition of "simple" structure among "imperfect" patterns and in their computational approach to arrive at such simple structures. As mentioned earlier, Thurstone's criteria specify empirical conditions under which a simple structure can be identifed unambiguously. One of the empirical specifications is that there should be at least three variables clearly loading on each factor. But the definition of simple structure does not depend on this type of empirical requirement, and it is desirable to separate this definition from actually identifying simple structure in data analysis. This is true because in exploratory factor analysis the researcher will have to be satisfied with whatever variables are at hand, and will be forced to conceptualize what constitutes the simplest structure, before trying to give meaning to the factors.

Historically, a simple structure was first specified in terms of *reference axes*. Although an understanding of these is not absolutely necessary (owing to the development of oblique rotation methods that do not rely on the introduction of reference axes), we will briefly describe them, since many users of factor analysis may have to rely on computer programs that provide oblique rotation methods that depend on the introduction of such axes.

Recall from the previous volume that the initial factor loadings are no more than the projection of variables on the two axes—that is, the loadings are found by dropping lines from each point perpendicular to the two initial orthogonal axes, and reading the values of the intersecting points on the two axes. Also note that a simple structure would exist in this orthogonal solution if all the variables lie on the axes. Also note that in the orthogonal case the notion of simple structure implies that one set of points will have zero loadings (or zero projection) on the other axis or factor. This zero projection is precluded if the angle between the clusters is not orthogonal (i.e., not 90°). Given such an oblique angle, a new procedure is to set up another reference axis that is perpendicular to the hyperplane (in this two factor model it is simply a line) that passes through the cluster of points which one considers to be a primary factor axis. (See Figure 4.)

Thus, it is the same to examine either the condition that a cluster of variables all lie on a primary axis or that a cluster of variables have all zero projections on the reference axes. In our contrived two-common factor model (when examined from the error-free correlation matrix), it is the case that one set of variables, X_1, X_2, X_3, have zero projections or loadings on the reference axis R_2, and variables in another set have zero

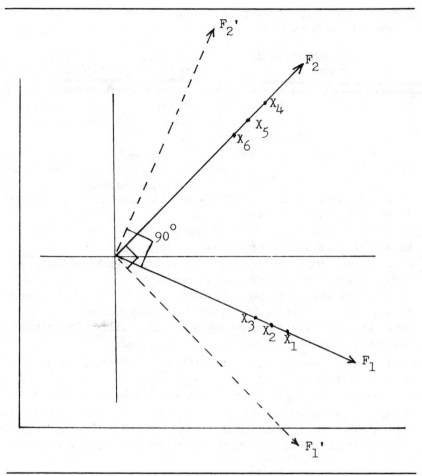

Figure 4: F_1 and F_2 are primary oblique factors and $F_1{}'$ and $F_2{}'$ are corresponding reference axes. The projections of X_1, X_2, and X_3 will be zero on $F_2{}'$, and the projections of X_4, X_5, and X_6 will be zero on $F_1{}'$.

loadings to R_1. In this example, it is not clear why one should rely on the reference axes instead of drawing lines directly through the cluster of variables. We merely note that when there are more than two factors and the clustering is not as clear as in the artificial data, the method of identifying reference axes, and treating these reference axes as if orthogonal axes in the next step or iteration, allows one to find a better fitting primary axis. What is important to remember from this is that the basic goal of the rotation is still to find a factor *pattern* matrix that is closest to the simplest ideal structure mentioned above.

Methods of Orthogonal Rotation:
Quartimax, Varimax, and Equimax

Since we assume the reader will have to depend on some existing factor analysis computer program when actually analyzing data, we will only describe basic principles which underlie each method. In the preceding section we described the simplest possible structure given k number of common factors and n number of variables. It is useful here to recapitulate some of the analytic properties of such a matrix.

Because each variable loads on only one factor, the factorial interpretation of *variables* is the simplest. But such a characterization is insufficient for expressing degrees of simplicity in numerical terms. One possible numerical measure of simplicity is the variability of the squared factor loadings for each row (or each variable). (We consider only squared loadings to avoid the problems of dealing with signs of the loadings.) Because variance is defined by the average of the squared deviations from the mean, the variance will be greatest (for a fixed number of factors and fixed communality) if one element of the squared loadings is equal to the communality, and all the rest in the row are zeros. In short, the maximum variance of the squared factor loadings for a variable is equivalent to the greatest simplicity of factorial complexity for that variable. It is, therefore, reasonable to quantify the notion of factorial simplicity by:

$$\text{Factorial Complexity of a Variable i} = \frac{1}{r} \sum_{j=1}^{r} (b_{ij}^2 - \bar{b}_{ij}^2)^2, \qquad [19]$$

where r is the number of columns in a pattern matrix, b_{ij} is the factor loading of variable i on the factor j, and $\bar{b}_{ij}^2$ is the mean of squared factor loadings for the row. Equation 19 can be written in the following form:

$$q_i = \frac{\sum_{j=1}^{r} (b_{ij}^4) - \left(\sum_{j=1}^{r} b_{ij}^2 \right)^2}{r^2} \qquad [20]$$

Once an initial factor solution is given, both r and the communality of each variable are fixed. Hence, the term after the minus sign remains fixed because

$$\sum_{j=1}^{r} b_{ij}^2 = h_i^2$$

in an orthogonal solution. Then the overall measure of simplicity can be obtained by summing q_i for all the variables:

$$q = \sum_{i=1}^{n} q_i = \sum_{i=1}^{n} \frac{\sum_{j=1}^{r} (b_{ij}^4) - \left(\sum_{j=1}^{r} b_{ij}^2\right)^2}{r^2}. \qquad [21]$$

Application of the *quartimax* criterion results in rotating axes in such a way that the factor loadings maximize q. Maximization of q is, however, equivalent to the maximization of the following terms,

$$Q = \sum_{i=1}^{n} \sum_{j=1}^{r} b_{ij}^4, \qquad [22]$$

because the remaining terms in equation 21 are all constants. Hence, the name quartimax.

In practice, application of this criterion may result in emphasizing the simplicity of interpretation of variables at the expense of simplicity of interpretation of factors. In particular, the interpretation of a variable becomes simpler as fewer common factors are involved in it, whereas the interpretations of a factor will be simpler if a relatively small number of variables have high loadings on the factor and the rest of the variables have zero loadings on it. In general, the quartimax criterion tends to produce final solutions in which there is a general factor with moderate and small loadings on some variables.

The *varimax* rotation uses a slightly different criterion which simplifies each column of the factor matrix. Instead of maximizing variance of squared loadings for each variable, it maximizes the variance of the squared loadings for each factor. The quantity to maximize—the index of simplicity of a factor j—is then:

$$v_j = \frac{n \sum_{i=1}^{n} b_{ij}^4 - \left(\sum_{i=1}^{n} b_{ij}^2\right)^2}{n^2} \qquad [23]$$

Note that now the sum is over n variables and that the term after the minus sign

$$(\sum_{j=1}^{n} b_{ij}^2)$$

does not remain fixed as does the corresponding term in equation 20. The overall measure of simplicity is given by

$$V = \sum_{j=1}^{r} v_j = \frac{\sum\limits_{j=1}^{r} n \sum\limits_{i=1}^{n} b_{ij}{}^4 - \left(\sum\limits_{i=1}^{n} b_{ij}{}^2\right)^2}{n^2} , \qquad [24]$$

which is known as the *row* varimax criterion. It is customary to use normalized factor loadings during the iterations in order to minimize the undesirable predominance of larger initial loadings for the resulting solution. Such a criterion is obtained if one uses b_{ij}^2/h_i^2 in the place of b_{ij}^2 in equation 24 and b_{ij}^4/h_i^4 in the place of b_{ij}^4.

In Table 6 we present the results of applying quartimax and varimax (normalized) rotations to the same data. We note that although the quartimax solution is analytically simpler than the varimax solution, the varimax seemed to give clearer separation of the factors. In general, Kaiser's experiment (1958) showed that the factor pattern obtained by varimax rotation tends to be more invariant than that obtained by the quartimax when different subsets of variables are factor analyzed.

Considering that the quartimax criterion concentrates on simplifying the rows and the varimax criterion concentrates on simplying the columns of the factor matrix, it is logical to consider applying both criteria with some appropriate weights. A general criterion is given by:

$$\alpha Q + \beta V = \text{Maximum}, \qquad [25]$$

where Q is given by equation 22 and V by equation 24 (but multiplied by n for convenience in manipulation and because a constant multiplier does not affect the maximization process), and α and β are weights. This may be written out

$$\sum_{j=1}^{r} \left(\sum_{i=1}^{n} b_{ij}{}^2\right)^2 - \gamma \left(\sum_{i=1}^{n} b_{ij}{}^2\right)^2/n = \text{maximum}, \qquad [26]$$

where $\gamma = \beta/(\alpha + \beta)$.

If $\gamma = 0$, it reduces to the quartimax criterion; if $\gamma = 1$, it reduces to the varimax criterion. When $\gamma = r/2$, it is called *equimax*, and when $\gamma = .5$, it is called *biquartimax*.

TABLE 6
Varimax and Quartimax Rotations Applied to the Same
Pattern Matrix Shown in Table 4[a]

Variables	Varimax Rotation		Quartimax Rotation	
	F_1	F_2	F_1	F_2
X_1	.787	.167	.793	.133
X_2	.730	.170	.736	.143
X_3	.595	.187	.602	.166
X_4	.154	.539	.173	.533
X_5	.083	.783	.111	.780
X_6	.306	.503	.324	.492

a. In this particular example, the tendency for the first factor in the Quartimax rotation to be a "general" factor is very slight.

Methods of Oblique Rotation

An oblique rotation is more general than an orthogonal rotation in that it does not arbitrarily impose the restriction that factors be uncorrelated. Its advantage over orthogonal rotations is that, after making oblique rotations, if the resulting factors are orthogonal, one can be sure that the orthogonality is not an artifact of the method of rotation. However, because oblique solutions are obtained with the introduction of correlations among factors, a different type of complexity in the interpretation of factor analysis may be introduced. In particular, one may have to assume higher-order factorial causation to explain correlations among the factors. Furthermore, there are two different types of approaches to oblique rotation—one using reference axes and the other using the primary pattern matrix. Since the overall principles for achieving simple structure were discussed in the previous sections, our descriptions of these will be brief.

SOLUTIONS BASED ON REFERENCE AXES

All the solutions included here are based on the fact that if there are definable clusters of variables representing separate dimensions, and if these clusters are correctly identified by primary factors, each cluster of variables will have near-zero projections on all reference axes but one. Therefore, a criterion similar to the quartimax can be defined as a *quartimin criterion:*

$$N = \sum_{i=1}^{n} \sum_{j<k=1}^{r} a_{ij}^2 \, a_{ik}^2 , \qquad [27]$$

where a_{ij} and a_{ik} are projections on the jth and the kth reference axes. This value will be zero if all the variables are unifactorial. But what we seek in the oblique rotation is factor loadings that will minimize N. (In orthogonal rotations, this criterion is equivalent to the quartimax.)

Parallel to the Varimax modification of the quartimax criterion in orthogonal rotations, there is a *covarimin* or *biquartimin* criterion. The minimized value in this case is the covariance of squared elements of the projections on the reference axes:

$$C = \sum_{j<k=1}^{r} \left(n \sum_{i=1}^{n} a_{ij}^2 \, a_{ik}^2 - \sum_{i=1}^{n} a_{ij}^2 \sum_{i=1}^{n} a_{ik}^2 \right) \qquad [28]$$

Once again, a version based on normalized values is obtained if we replace a_{ij}^2 with a_{ij}^2 / h_i^2. When applied to the same set of data, the covarimin criterion tends to produce fewer oblique factors while the quartimin criterion produces more oblique factors.

Given the opposite tendencies shown by these two criteria, it is natural to combine them. The most general version is given by:

$B = \alpha N + \beta C / n = $ minimum where α and β are weights to   [29]
be assigned and N and C are given above.

By multiplying equation 29 by n, combining the terms, and setting $\gamma = \beta/(\alpha + \beta)$, we get the general *oblimin* criterion:

$$B = \sum_{j<k=1}^{r} \left(n \sum_{i=1}^{n} a_{ij}^2 \, a_{ik}^2 - \gamma \sum_{i=1}^{n} a_{ij}^2 \sum_{i=1}^{n} a_{ik}^2 \right). \qquad [30]$$

This general criterion reduces to:

Quartimin when $\gamma = 0$ (most oblique)
Biquartimin when $\gamma = .5$ (less oblique)
Covarimin where $\gamma = 1$ (least oblique).

We note once again that it is customary to use the normalized oblimin criterion by replacing a_{ij}^2 with a_{ij}^2/h_i^2.

Another criterion closely related to the principles specified in developing oblimin, but based on completely different algorithms, is the binormamin criterion. This is an attempt to objectify the choice of γ in equation 30 as a means of correcting for the "too oblique" bias of quartimin and for the "too orthogonal" bias of covarimin. Compared to biquartimin, which adopts $1/2$ for γ, the binormamin is reported to be more satisfactory if the data are either particularly simple or particularly complex.

SOLUTIONS BASED ON THE
FACTOR PATTERN WITH DIRECT OBLIMIN

In recent years, Jennrich and Sampson (1966) developed a criterion which is based on simplifying loadings on the primary factors (not reference axes) and introduced a successful computer program. The value minimized is defined as exactly parallel to equation 30, with the only difference being the use of primary factor loadings (loadings in the pattern matrix) in the place of loadings on the reference axes. The criterion is:

$$D = \sum_{j=k=1}^{r} \left[\sum_{i=1}^{n} b_{ij}^2 b_{ik}^2 - d\left(\sum_{i=1}^{n} b_{ij}^2 \sum_{i=1}^{n} b_{ik}^2 \right) / n \right], \quad [31]$$

where b_{ij} are factor loadings in a pattern matrix, with the slight difference between D and B being the division of the terms by n in D. As in indirect oblimin, the researcher can modify the degree of obliqueness of the final solution by the choice of d in equation 31.

In general, greater values of d produce more oblique solutions and smaller (negative) values produce more orthogonal solutions. If the factor pattern is unifactorial (the simplest possible), the specification of d = 0 identifies the correct pattern.

A word of caution is necessary here. Although the formula is similar, choice of d in direct oblimin does not have a known correspondence with the choice of γ in indirect oblimin. To gain a better understanding of the effects of specifying a different d, the reader may consult Harman (1975).

OTHER METHODS OF OBLIQUE ROTATION

There are many additional methods of oblique rotation. We will identify a few of the better known solutions.

The *oblimax* criterion (Saunders, 1953) is based on an attempt to simplify the structure by maximizing the number of small and large loadings at the expense of medium loadings. As an objective criterion, it finds a solution which maximizes the kurtosis of doubled factor loadings. (The doubling is done by counting each loading twice, one with the original sign and the other with the reversed one.) This criterion is equivalent to quartimax in orthogonal rotation but leads to a different solution from quartimin (the oblique counterpart of quartimax) when used without restricting to orthogonal axes.

Two more rotation methods need be mentioned at least in passing. Harris and Kaiser's orthoblique method (1964) is gaining wider use, and the Maxplane Method (Cattel and Muerle, 1960; Eber, 1966) is a possible alternative because it is based on a somewhat different criterion of fit than all the others so far examined.

Rotation to a Target Matrix

Instead of applying rotation methods to achieve some analytically defined simple structure, it is possible and sometimes desirable to rotate factors in order to fit a specific simple structure the researcher has in mind or has hypothesized to exist.

The first possibility is that the researcher specifies the exact loadings on each variable, and then makes rotations either with orthogonal restrictions or without such restrictions in such a way that the fit between the specified matrix and the final rotated factor matrix is minimum according to the least squares criterion. This type of rotation is usually performed to examine the congruity of a one factor structure to another factor structure which is already known or presented elsewhere.

The second approach, known as *promax* oblique rotation, is simply a way of obtaining an oblique solution by using some functions of the orthogonal solution as the target matrix (Hendrickson and White, 1964). The rationale behind the promax rotation is that the orthogonal solutions are usually close to the oblique solution, and by reducing the smaller loadings to near-zero loadings, one can obtain a reasonably good simple structure target matrix. Then by finding the best fitting oblique factors for this target matrix, one obtains the desired oblique solution. There are different algorithms for solving for the target structure matrix and for the target pattern matrix, but we will not describe them.

TABLE 7
Target Matrix with Os and 1s

Variables	Factors	
	1	2
X_1	1	0
X_2	1	0
X_3	1	0
X_4	0	1
X_5	0	1
X_6	0	1

The third and more general approach is to use a target matrix which is less specific than the preceding ones. Instead of making a least squares fit to a target matrix in which all the values are exactly specified, one may simply specify 0s and 1s. This is the most realistic target matrix in that we usually do not know the exact values to expect, but have some notion about which loadings should be high and which should be low. An example of such a target matrix is given in Table 7.

Such a target matrix can be modified to make it even more general: some are specified to be zero, some are specified to be some other fixed values, and the remainder are left to vary freely. This will be more thoroughly discussed in the section on confirmatory factor analysis.

IV. NUMBER OF FACTORS PROBLEM REVISITED

Although we previously examined various methods of initial factoring, where the objective is to find the minimum number of factors compatible with the data, there are several reasons to reexamine this issue. First, in discussing the initial factoring methods, we essentially assumed that the number of factors question could be resolved without ambiguity, and therefore, did not discuss various technical points pertaining to this question. Second, some of the initial solutions are not satisfactory as a means for answering this question, thus requiring that rotated solutions be examined. Third, we must contend with the problems caused by an imperfect fit between the factor analytic model and the data. Fourth, most existing computer programs will require the user to provide some information regarding the number of factors question, and we want to prepare the reader for this contingency.

There are several rules typically applied in addressing the number of factors question. Some of these are distinct alternatives while some are complementary to each other. The most important rules involve: (1) significance tests associated with the maximum likelihood and least squares solutions, (2) varieties of the eigenvalue criterion, (3) the criterion of substantive importance, (4) the Scree-test, and (5) the criterion of interpretability and invariance.

Significance Tests

The large sample χ^2-test associated with the maximum likelihood solution is the most satisfactory solution from a purely statistical point of view, provided that the assumptions of the method are adequately met. Application of the method has shown that for a large sample with many variables, the number of factors retained tends to be much larger than the number of factors the researcher is willing to accept. Although this really is not a defect of the method, it has forced researchers to also apply another criterion—that of substantive significance, which is applied after finding statistical significance.

Monte Carlo experiments usually show that the maximum likelihood criterion is most appropriate when applied to known population models without substantively insignificant minor factors. That is, it is an efficient method to deal with sampling variability, but it is not the best when minor deviations are built into the model. Given sufficient sample size, any of these deviations will be treated as "significant" dimensions that cannot be accounted for by sampling variability. This implies, therefore, that it may be preferable on substantive grounds to ignore some minor factors after proper rotation.

Although we described the use of this method as a fail-safe procedure under which the adequacy of a one-common factor model is tested, and then the adequacy of the two factor model if the data deviate "significantly" from the one factor model, and so on, such a procedure is often too costly to use on large sets of variables. Therefore, one may combine one of the quick methods of determining the number of common factors (to be described below) with the maximum likelihood test. After making the initial "guess" of significant factors, one may increase the number if the data deviate significantly from the assumed model, *or* decrease the number if the initial model is accepted as adequate (to make sure that one has the minimum number of factors that are compatible with the data). From a statistical point of view, the least squares solution is not as efficient as maximum likelihood but the same comments apply to this solution.

Eigenvalue Specification

One of the most popular criteria for addressing the number of factors question is to retain factors with eigenvalues greater than 1 when the correlational (not adjusted) matrix is decomposed. This simple criterion seems to work well, in the sense that it generally gives results consistent with researchers' expectations, and it works well when applied to samples from artifically created population models.

In a population correlation matrix, such a criterion will always establish a lower-bound for the number of common factors. That is, the number of common factors responsible for the correlation matrix will always be equal or greater than the number specified by this criterion. However, this strict inequality need not hold when the sample correlation matrix is considered. Although Kaiser provides several reasons for its success, its acceptance is still based on heuristic and practical grounds. After examining other more "sophisticated" criteria, Kaiser still favors this one (Kaiser, 1974).

Another related eigenvalue criterion is that of retaining vectors with eigenvalues greater than zero when the reduced correlation matrix (with squared multiple Rs in the main diagonal) is decomposed. The rationale behind this criterion is that in a population correlation matrix, it provides an even stricter lower-bound for the number of common factors responsible for the data. But the same may not necessarily apply to the sample correlation matrix, and application to empirical data usually produces more factors than normally accepted on other grounds.

When the communalities are estimated and inserted in the main diagonal, this eigenvalue criterion can be applied. However, when some of the eigenvalues are negative, as will usually be the case, it does not make sense to extract all the factors with the eigenvalues greater than zero. Although the sum of both negative and positive eigenvalues is the same as the sum of all communalities (or variances explained by common factors), the negative values are not meaningfully interpreted within the context of variance, and their presence makes the sum of positive eigenvalues "inflated" in the sense that their sum is greater than the sum of the communalities. Harman (1975:141) suggests that one should stop extracting common factors before the cumulative sum of eigenvalues exceeds the sum of the estimated communalities.

Criterion of Substantive Importance

Considering that the "significance" tests focus on sampling variability and the eigenvalue criterion focuses on some abstract properties of a matrix, a third alternative to use is to focus directly on the criterion of what should be considered a minimum contribution by a factor to be evaluated as substantively significant. This criterion is easy to understand when the initial factoring is based on the decomposition of the unaltered correlation matrix; the proportion to specify is the proportion of the total variance (which is the number of variables) to be explained by the last factor to be retained. (Recall that in every extraction method we discussed, the initial factors were arranged in the order of their magnitude.) One may set the criterion at whatever level is considered substantively important. Some possibilities are one percent, five percent, or ten percent. However, note that the use of "eigenvalue 1" criterion is equivalent to setting the minimum variance explained at $(100/n)$ percent level.

On the other hand, when the altered correlation matrix is factored, as is done in every method we discussed except for principal components, the proportion to specify is the proportion of the last eigenvalue relative to the sum of the eigenvalues (sum of the main diagonal of the matrix to be factored). The major disadvantage of the method is that it uses a subjective criterion. The obvious advantage is that the researcher who is not familiar with the properties of eigenvalue decomposition of a matrix may rely on a measure of relative magnitude which "appears" easier to interpret.

Scree-Test

This is a test advocated by Cattell (1965). The rule directs one to examine the graph of eigenvalues, and stop factoring at the point where the eigenvalues (or characteristic roots) begin to level off forming a straight line with an almost horizontal slope. Beyond this point Cattell describes the smooth slope as "factorial litter or scree" (where scree is the geological term referring to the debris which collects on the lower part of a rocky slope). Its use is illustrated in Figure 5. Based on these results, the re-

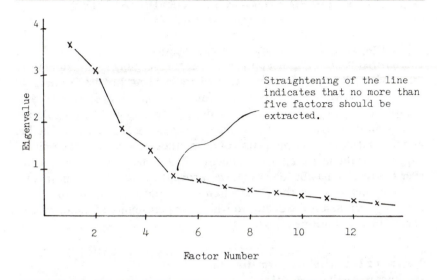

Figure 5: Illustration of Scree-Test

searcher would conclude that not more than five factors should be extracted.

Some Monte Carlo studies indicate that this method is often superior to others where there are minor factors and the interest is in locating only major common factors (Tucker, Koopman and Linn, 1969; Linn, 1968). Some, like Kaiser (1970), argue that this "root-staring" criterion is often very subjective because it is not uncommon to find more than one major break in the root-graph and there is no unambiguous rule to use.

Criteria of Interpretability and Invariance

As a way to protect oneself from accepting results which are dubious, a general rule-of-thumb is to try to combine various rules, accept only those conclusions that are supported by several independent criteria, and consider others as tentative hypotheses (Harris, 1967). Given the complexity as well as uncertainties inherent in the method, the final judgment has to rest on the reasonableness of the solution on the basis of current standards of scholarship in one's own field. This criterion is elusive but, fortunately or unfortunately, all of us must live with it in order to communicate our findings to our fellow scientists.

V. INTRODUCTION TO CONFIRMATORY
FACTOR ANALYSIS

Thus far we have concentrated on exploratory factor analysis and have emphasized the fact that in applying the technique, numerous assumptions must be made, the most important of these being the assumptions of factorial causation and parsimony. Since all one does in this type of analysis is to impose a particular model on the data and find a solution that is most compatible with the data, one can legitimately ask whether and to what extent the application of the method generates some empirical support for the factor analytic model itself. As mentioned earlier, whatever the results may be, one can never prove the existence of a particular causal structure from the observation of the covariance structure. One can, however, assess the degree to which the plausibility of factor models is empirically confirmed.

Degree of Empirical Confirmation for
the Factor Analytic Model

Compared to exploratory factor analysis, we introduce more specific hypotheses about the factor structure in confirmatory factor analysis and, therefore, the chance that such specific hypotheses will be supported by a given covariance structure is smaller, if in fact some factorial causation is not in operation. In that sense, most confirmatory factor analysis can provide self-validating information. If a given factorial hypothesis is supported by the data, we will in general also have greater confidence in the appropriateness of the factor analytic model for the given data. (Of course, the degree to which such empirical confirmation is provided varies from one analysis to another.) Moreover, even a purely exploratory analysis can provide us with varying degrees of self-validating information. Before introducing confirmatory factor analysis, therefore, it is important to discuss the notion of empirical confirmation in general, and some of the means by which we assess whether or not we have data that are appropriate for factor analysis.

AN ILLUSTRATION

Applying the factor analytical model to a bivariate correlation does not generate information other than what is already known by the researcher. This is so because a one-common factor model is always compatible with a bivariate correlation. Hence, factor analysis is never applied to this situation, not because a factor analytic model is incompatible with the data but because the degree of empirical confirmation of the model (to be called informativeness for short) is zero, and because (though much more trivial) there is no unique solution. Consider the relationship between the first two variables in the model shown in Figure 1. Given any correlation one can arbitrarily choose one factor loading to be between −1 and +1 (except 0) and still find the other factor loading which will be compatible with the observed correlation. In short, there always is a factor solution compatible with data.

The situation changes slightly when factor analysis is applied to a three variable correlation matrix. If one finds that a one-common factor model is compatible with the data, the degree of empirical confirmation obtained is not zero, because some random correlation matrices will not be compatible with a one-common factor model. In particular, for a three variable correlation matrix to be compatible with a one-common factor model the relationships among the three correlation coefficients must meet the conditions that (1) all the correlations are positive or only an even number of them can be negative, and (2) the magnitude of any one coefficient be equal to or greater than the magnitude of the product of the remaining two coefficients:

$$|r_{ij}| \geqslant |r_{ik}r_{jk}|. \qquad [32]$$

It is informative to derive the condition specified by equation 32. Consider Figure 18 in the previous volume (or the upper half of Figure 1), and recall that

$$r_{12} = b_1b_2 \qquad h_1 = b_1^2$$

$$r_{13} = b_1b_3 \quad \text{and} \quad h_2 = b_2^2$$

$$r_{23} = b_2b_3 \qquad h_3 = b_3^2.$$

Next, let us multiply two correlation coefficients as follows:

$$r_{12}r_{13} = b_1b_2b_1b_3 = b_1^2b_2b_3 = h_1^2r_{23}. \qquad [33]$$

The term after the first equal sign is given by expressing the correlations in terms of factor loadings, the terms after the second sign by rearranging, and the last terms are given by substituting corresponding communalities and correlations for the factor loadings. A slight rearrangement of equation 33 and the fact that communalities cannot be greater than 1 leads to the condition specified by equation 32:

$$h^2 = r_{12}r_{13}/r_{23} \leqslant 1,$$

which implies that $|r_{23}| \geq |r_{12}r_{13}|$. In general, all the three variable one-common factor models must meet the condition that $|r_{ij}| \geq |r_{ik}r_{jk}|$. To the extent that not all the randomly produced correlation matrices of three variables would satisfy the above condition, finding that one's data meet the requirement of a one-common factor model is informative, but not highly informative because many random matrices can be compatible with the one-common factor model. In other words, the condition specified by equation 32 is met by many random matrices of three correlations.

Recall from Section II of the first volume that a four variable correlation matrix based on a one-common factor model meets three additional conditions, namely:

$$r_{13}r_{24} = r_{14}r_{23} \qquad\qquad [34]$$

$$r_{12}r_{34} = r_{14}r_{23}$$

$$r_{13}r_{24} = r_{12}r_{34}$$

This rule is easy to derive and remember because, using an example, $r_{13}r_{24} = b_1b_3b_2b_4 = (b_1b_4)(b_2b_3) = r_{14}r_{23}$. (The same procedure is employed as in deriving the inequality condition in equation 32.) In general, then, the greater the number of variables, the greater the number of conditions that the correlation matrix has to meet to satisfy the requirements of a particular factor model. Therefore, the fact that a one-common factor model is compatible with a four variable matrix provides the researcher some empirical confirmation that the factor analytic assumption may not be totally arbitrary.

Thus, a factor analytic result can provide some empirical confirmation about the appropriateness of the model itself, in the sense that only when certain constraints are met by the correlation matrix can a given factor model fit the data. Furthermore, the greater the ratio of the number of variables to the number of hypothesized factors, the greater the empirical confirmation of the factor analytic model, because it implies that a greater number of structural constraints do indeed exist in the correlation matrix in order to satisfy the factor analytic model.

Now recall that applying factor analysis implies imposing various assumptions on the data. It is possible then to reject the factor analytic model purely on the grounds that these assumptions are arbitrary or inappropriate. However, one must temper such a judgment when the degree of empirical confirmation is high, because one has to account for the existence of structural constraints in the data (i.e., lack of randomness). Viewed from a slightly different perspective, it can be said that the informativeness of factor analysis varies from application to application;

results of some factor analysis can be much more informative than those of others. Still another way of looking at it is that factor analysis *can* provide self-validating information; the greater the number of empirical constraints a given solution must satisfy, the greater the degree of our confidence in the appropriateness of the factor analytic model for the data. Therefore, depending on the outcome, even an exploratory factor analysis can provide some empirical confirmation about the appropriateness and the economy of the model.

Number of Empirical Constraints Implied by a Model

Given the preceding discussion, it is important to know the number of empirical constraints implied by a given factor model (the number of conditions to be met by a correlation matrix in order to fit a particular model). Fortunately, the number is equivalent to the number of degrees of freedom associated with the significance test for the maximum likelihood solution. (A careful examination of this number is instructive because a clear understanding of the relationship between a factorial hypothesis and the implied degrees of freedom is crucial for the understanding of confirmatory factor analysis to be discussed shortly.)

There are, however, several different ways to specify the number of constraints for a correlation matrix implied by a particular factor model. One way to approach the problem is to use the rank-theorem, which states that if correct-communalities are inserted in the correlation matrix (produced by an r-common factor model), the rank (or number of independent dimensions) of the adjusted correlation matrix will be r, which in turn implies that all the submatrices which contain more than r columns and r rows will have zero determinants. From this, one can specify the number of conditions a correlation matrix must satisfy for a given number of factors and variables (e.g., Harman, 1976). The other approach is to examine the degrees of freedom in the context of a significance test. Because the first approach leads to the same number of conditions specified by application of a significance test, we will derive it in the more general context of the second approach.

To illustrate, assume we begin with an empirical correlation matrix. The amount of independent information contained in such a matrix is $(1/2) n (n-1)$—the number of cells in the upper triangle. Given such data, factor analysis arrives at an initial solution by allowing n x r (where r is the number of common factors) factor loadings to vary in such a way that these loadings best reproduce the observed correlation matrix. But in initial factoring, we require these n x r factor loadings to satisfy the condition that the resulting factors are orthogonal. This implies that

TABLE 8
Degrees of Freedom Associated with n Variables and r Factors[a]

Number of Variables (n)	Number of Factors				Maximum Number of Factors With Positive Degrees of Freedom	Number of Independent Coefficients $\frac{1}{2}n(n-1)$
	1	2	3	4		
3	0	-2	-3	--	none	3
4	2	-1	-3	-4	1	6
5	5	1	-2	-4	2	10
6	9	4	0	-3	2	15
7	14	8	3	-1	3	21
8	20	13	7	2	4	28
9	27	19	12	6	5	36
10	35	26	18	11	5	45
11	44	34	25	17	6	55
12	54	43	33	24	7	66
20	170	151	133	116	14	190
40	740	701	663	626	31	780

a. The general formula is $D = \dfrac{(n-r)^2 - (n+r)}{2}$ = the number of constraints to be satisfied by the data.

$1/2r(r-1)$ arbitrary conditions are imposed. Consequently, we will use the following number of free parameters in arriving at the initial factor solution:

$$nr - (1/2)r(r-1). \qquad [35]$$

Therefore, the number of conditions that an empirical correlation matrix has to satisfy independently of the model is the difference:

Number of Empirical $= 1/2n(n-1) - [nr - 1/2r(r-1)]$ [36]
Constraints Required
$$= 1/2[(n-r)^2 - (n+r)],$$

which is the same as the degrees of freedom presented earlier. (When a *covariance* matrix is used in the place of a correlation matrix, the amount of independent information contained in the matrix is $1/2n(n+1)$ instead of $1/2n(n-1)$. However, the final degrees of freedom remains the same because of the additional impositions necessary for the factor analysis model to be applied to the covariance matrix.)

In order to gain some familiarity with what is implied by equation 36, we present in Table 8 actual values for various combinations of number of factors and variables. There are several aspects to note. First, the number of empirical constraints to be satisfied increase, in general, as the ratio of the number of variables to the number of factors increases. Second, when the number is negative, a factor analytic result would not provide any empirical confirmation of the model. Hence, it makes sense in general to consider only those factor models that require some empirical constraints in the data. For example, applying a two-common factor model to a four variable matrix or a three factor model to a matrix with six or less number of variables would not be informative. Third, the number of required constraints increases rapidly as the number of variables increases for a fixed number of factors. Therefore, the addition of a variable to the factor analysis can add a great deal more empirical content to factor analytic results. Fourth, if one uses this number as an index of the empirical confirmation, it would seem to imply that what is really important is not the ratio, but the difference between the number of variables and the number of common factors hypothesized. Notice that the number of constraints to be satisfied is almost the same among the following combinations: 1 factor with 7 variables (14); 2 factors with 8 variables (13); 3 factors with 9 variables (12), and so on. But there is no reason to consider this index to be a direct measure of the degree of empirical confirmation. One alternative is to examine the ratio of (a) the number of constraints to be satisfied to (b) the number of independent coefficients in the observed matrix. Although we do not present these ratios in the table (the base number is given in the last column), we note that such a measure would indicate that the ratio of variables to factors would be more important than the raw index would indicate.

There are two complications that must be taken into consideration in assessing the degree of empirical confirmation provided by factor solutions. The first complication is that the requirements, even if they are met exactly in the population, are not likely to be met exactly in the sample. The second is that even in the population, the factor analytic model may not exactly fit the data; hence, the requirements have to be evaluated taking minor misfits into consideration. The most frustrating part is that in actual analysis there is no way of separating one complication from the other. In practice, therefore, one cannot use equation 36 alone as a measure of empirical confirmation. Given some degree of fit between a factor solution and observed data, a solution which has to meet a greater number of empirical constraints would provide greater confirmation. But to be able to assess that, one must find a way of evaluating the fit.

DEGREE OF EMPIRICAL CONFIRMATION OR RELIABILITY

A significance test associated with some initial factoring methods assesses the degree to which the discrepancy between the hypothesized model and observed data can be attributed to the sampling variability. The significance test is directly dependent upon the sample size; given a sufficiently large sample, any discrepancy between the model and observed data can be made significant. This is the result of the fact that if a factor model fits exactly the population data, the greater the sample size, the smaller the discrepancy between the population values and sample statistic. When sample size is very large, the deviation should be very small.

This statistical principle runs into trouble whenever the researcher suspects the existence of minor factors, and is unwilling or unable to specify their exact nature. In such a case, the significance test may not reveal the adequacy of the model—that is, even if the specified factor model is economical in that it explains a large portion of the observed covariance and brings some order to the data structure, the test may indicate that the model is statistically inadequate. Therefore, we need a descriptive index of adequacy of the factor model, which is conceptually independent of statistical significance.

The statistic we need is a measure of discrepancy between the observed correlation matrix and the reproduced matrix. One possibility, suggested by Harman, is to use the residual-mean-square, in which the squared deviations between the observed correlations and predicted correlations (by the final factor solution) are summed and divided by the number of cells under consideration:

$$\sum_{i \neq j} \sum (r_{ij} - \hat{r}_{ij})^2 / [n(n-1)],$$

where the summation is over all the off-diagonal elements (Harman, 1976:176). This measure, however, does not have a convenient upper limit against which to interpret its relative magnitude.

Another alternative is Tucker and Lewis's reliability coefficient (1973) for the maximum likelihood factor solution. The measure is based on the residual correlations in the matrix after the effects of final factors are taken out; it is therefore ultimately based on the fit between the observed correlations and correlations based on the factor solution. Their reliability coefficient incorporates, however, two additional adjustments: it divides the overall discrepancy by the degrees-of-freedom, thereby adjusting for the potential differences between factor solutions, and it compares the adjusted measure of deviation with the comparable deviation when factors are assumed not operative, thereby making it a measure of proportional reduction in adjusted discrepancy. The coefficient, therefore, ranges between 0 and 1, the former representing the poorest fit and the latter a complete fit. An abbreviated formula is:

$$\text{rho} = \frac{M_o - M_k}{M_o} \qquad [37]$$

where M_0 = Expected χ^2 in the absence of factor effect divided by $(1/2)$ $n(n-k1)$, M_k = χ^2 for the final solution divided by $(1/2)\,[(n-r)^2 - (n+r)]$. (See also Sörbom and Jöreskog, 1976:4-5). A more useful, but less accurate, description of the formula which converges to equation 37 as sample size gets larger is:

$$\text{Approximate rho} = 1 - \frac{E_1}{E_2}$$

$$\text{where } E_1 = \sum_{i=j} \sum (r_{ij \cdot F})^2/df_k \text{ and}$$

$$E_2 = \sum_{i=j} \sum (r_{ij})^2/\,[1/2\,n(n-1)]\,,$$

where $r_{ij \cdot F}$ is the partial correlation among variables after the effects of k-factors are taken out, and df, is the degree of freedom, which will be $1/2[(n-r)^2 - (n+r)]$ in an exploratory factor analysis, but will be a larger number in confirmatory factor analysis. (The residual partial correlation is no more than a standardized version of the discrepancy between the predicted correlations and observed ones.)

Another Conception of Empirical Confirmation: Sampling Adequacy

The conventional statistical tests assume only the sampling of units (objects or entities), but in practice we cannot ignore the fact that a certain degree of psychometric sampling is involved—the variables we analyze are almost always a subset of a potentially larger domain of relevant variables. One must then ask whether the given data (subset of variables) are adequate for factor analysis. (The reader may recall that image factoring and alpha factoring assume such psychometric sampling, but the issue is relevant for any type of factor analysis.)

In general, it is true that other things being equal, the degree of empirical confirmation is greater if (1) the number of variables increases, (2) the number of common factor decreases, (3) the residual correlations decrease, or (4) the greater the degree of factorial determination. The first two conditions are directly related to the increase in the empirical constraints imposed on the data by the factorial model, the third condition measures the degree to which a factor model accounts for the observed covariation, and the last one specifies that the variance of each variable be accounted for mostly by common factors. The last condition is directly related to the notion of sampling adequacy, because the degree of overall factorial determination will increase, other things being equal, with an increase in the number of variables and with an increase in the average magnitude of correlations.

The rule-of-thumb index of sampling adequacy is proposed by Kaiser (1970, 1974), which he calls an overall "measure of sampling adequacy."

$$\text{MSA} = \frac{\sum\limits_{j \neq k} \sum r_{jk}^2}{\sum\limits_{j \neq k} \sum r_{jk}^2 + \sum\limits_{j \neq k} \sum q_{ik}^2} \qquad [38]$$

where r_{ij} is an original correlation and q_{ij} is an element of the anti-image correlation matrix, which is given by $Q = SR^{-1}S$, where R^{-1} is an inverse of the correlation matrix and $S = (\text{diag } R^{-1})^{1/2}$. The index ranges between 0 and 1. In fact, the index becomes 1 if and only if all the off-diagonal elements of the inverse of the correlation matrix are zero, which in turn implies that every variable can be predicted without error from other variables in the set. The guide for interpreting the measure is as follows (Kaiser, 1974):

in the .90's	marvelous
in the .80's	meritorious
in the .70's	middling
in the .60's	mediocre
in the .50's	miserable
below .50	unacceptable.

Kaiser claims that extensive experience with data shows that the magnitude of MSA improves as (1) the number of variables increases,

(2) the number of common factors decreases, (3) the number of cases (entities) increases, and (4) the average magnitude of correlations increases (1970).

To recapitulate, the degree to which data provide empirical evidence that a given factor analytic model is appropriate for the problem at hand varies from one situation to another. The researcher should be aware of the conditions that improve the informativeness of factor analysis. Furthermore, a novice to factor analysis may rely on a rule-of-thumb index such as Kaiser's MSA in order to acquire a rough idea of whether the data are adequate for the technique. Of course, the ultimate decision must be made on the basis of theoretical justification.

Confirmatory Factor Analysis

The minimum requirement of any confirmatory factor analysis is that one hypothesize before hand the number of common factors. However, the hypothesis, if it is to be different from a hunch or guess, must be based on an understanding of the nature of the variables under consideration, as well as on expectations concerning which factor is likely to load on which variables. This cannot be overemphasized because the variety in the actual form of these factorial hypotheses is almost limitless.

We can classify confirmatory factor analysis into two general types: (1) one in which only one group or population is involved, and (2) another in which two or more groups or populations are involved. We begin with the first type.

ONE GROUP OR POPULATION

Given a covariance matrix for a group, in confirmatory factor analysis, one starts with an hypothesis about the factorial structure thought to be responsible for the observed covariance structure. Then one evaluates whether the observed data structure deviates "significantly" from the hypothesized structure. At one extreme, the hypothesis may specify: (a) the number of common factors, (b) the nature of the relationship among factors—either orthogonal or oblique, and (c) the magnitude of factor loadings for each variable. At the other extreme, the hypothesis may be no more than a specification about the number of underlying common factors. There are, of course, numerous possible hypotheses which lie between these extremes.

Because the simplest form of confirmatory factor analysis, where only the number of common factors is specified, is not very different from exploratory factor analysis, only brief comments are necessary. For this type of hypothesis, whether one employs an orthogonal or oblique factor model is immaterial, and a significance test or some other criterion (such as a reliability coefficient) which evaluates the adequacy of initial factor solutions is satisfactory. Therefore, the only difference to note here is that one starts with a number that is based on some prior consideration, whereas, in exploratory analysis one starts with a "safe" number and increments it if the first guess is not adequate. We should also mention that it may not be wise to rely completely on significance tests unless one is willing to accept substantively minor but statistically significant factors. If a judgmental criterion is also to be employed, it is desirable to rotate the solution and then determine whether the emerging structure is meaningful.

The other extreme is also easy to discuss. If the researcher has specific hypotheses about the number of factors, the nature of the relationships among factors, and the specific loadings, it is possible either to check whether the reproduced correlation matrix under the hypothesis is close enough to the observed correlations, or use the hypothesis as a target matrix and find a solution which approximates the target while maximally reproducing the observed correlations. In the former, the check of the adequacy of the hypothesis depends on some test for evaluating similarity between covariance matrices and, in the latter case, some test for evaluating similarity between two factor solutions is required. For more details, the readers may consult a volume in this series (Levine, 1977). In general, it is unrealistic to expect a researcher to possess hypotheses this specific in actual factor analysis. Nevertheless, such an hypothesis can arise if one is comparing the structure of one factor analysis (for one data set) with the structure based on other data. This is the case which can be subsumed under a more general solution to be discussed shortly.

Because Sörbom and Jöreskog's latest confirmatory factor program allows a great deal of flexibility, we will outline some of the important specification options available in that program (Sörbom and Jöreskog, 1976). There are several ways one can specify any parameter. The parameters involved in factor analysis are the factor loadings (nr for common factors) and the correlation coefficients among factors ($1/2 \ r(r-1)$). Any of these parameters can be *fixed* at a particular value or left free to vary. Usually, the most useful way of fixing a parameter would be to specify a particular loading to be zero. For example, if all the factor correlations are fixed to be zero, then an orthogonal solution is being specified. Another way of specifying parameters is to *constrain* a parameter to be equal to another parameter.

To make the preceding discussion more concrete we present in Table 9 three examples of specifying *free* and *fixed* parameters. In these examples, x's represent free parameters and zeros represent fixed parameters—fixed

TABLE 9
Three Examples of Specifying Parameters in
Confirmatory Factor Analysis[a]

Variables	Example 1 F_1	F_2	F_3	Example 2 F_1	F_2	F_3	Example 3 F_1	F_2	F_3
X_1	X	O	O	X	X	O	X	X	X
X_2	X	O	O	X	X	O	X	X	X
X_3	X	O	O	X	X	O	X	X	X
X_4	O	X	O	X	X	O	X	X	O
X_5	O	X	O	X	O	X	X	X	O
X_6	O	X	O	X	O	X	X	O	O
X_7	O	O	X	X	O	X	X	O	O
X_8	O	O	X	X	O	X	X	O	O

a. X represents free parameters; O represents parameters fixed to be zero.

to be zero. One could fix the parameters at other values, such as 1.0, .5, and so on, but we think it realistic only to expect the researcher to have some notion about where loadings should be high and where they should be low. The first hypothesis specifies a unifactorial structure—the simplest possible type given the number of variables, the second hypothesis antici- pates a general factor and two group factors, and the third specifies a special hierarchy. The researcher may, of course, introduce many modifi- cations in these patterns.

Along with the specifications illustrated above, one also has to specify the nature of the relationships among factors. The most usual forms of specifying them are: (1) specifying all the factor correlations to be zero— an orthogonal hypothesis, (2) allowing all the correlations to vary—an oblique hypothesis, or (3) a mixed pattern in which some are assumed to be orthogonal while leaving others to take any value.

An illustration of confirmatory factory analysis is presented in Table 10, using the sample data from Table 1. Suppose that the researcher is willing to hypothesize, (1) that there are two underlying common factors, (2) that the two factors can be correlated, and (3) that one factor has zero loadings on X_4, X_5, X_6 and the other factor has zero loadings on X_1, X_2, X_3.

Note that, compared to exploratory factor analysis, we are making 6 parameters (factorloadings) fixed out of 12 (nr), but making 1 parameter free in the *factor* covariance matrix. Consequently, we are imposing

TABLE 10
Fixed and Free Parameters Specified in Solving the
Oblique Factor Pattern[a]

Variables	Factors	
	F_1	F_2
X_1	X	0
X_2	X	0
X_3	X	0
X_4	0	X
X_5	0	X
X_6	0	X

Correlations Among Factors

	F_1	F_2
F_1	1	
F_2		1

a. Os indicate fixed parameters and Xs represent parameters which are free to vary. The 1s in factor correlation matrices can be considered fixed when the covariance matrix is input. However, in our calculation of degrees of freedom, we counted these values as part of the general specification, so we do not count 1s as fixed.

altogether 5 additional constraints. But not all of these 5 restrictions will be reflected in the increased degrees of freedom. In exploratory analysis, we also use $\frac{1}{2} r(r-1)$ implicit conditions in order to make a particular solution unique. Hence, the degrees of freedom increase is $5 - \frac{1}{2} r(r-1) = 4$. In general, the fit between the models with fixed parameters and the data will be poorer than the fit between the model without fixed parameters. But what is lost in terms of fit usually will be more than compensated for

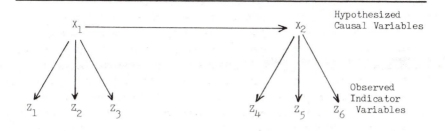

Figure 6: Causal Model Involving Two Hypothetical Variables and Indicator Variables

by the increased degrees of freedom, if the hypothesized model is appropriate.

Also note that it would not make much sense to apply a three-common factor model to a six variable matrix. However, it is quite possible to apply such a model to these data if the hypothesized factor structure has enough constraints to accommodate several degrees of freedom. An example would be: specify that X_1 and X_2 load only on factor 1, that X_3 and X_4 load only on factor 2, and X_5 and X_6 load only on factor 3.

We note that the principle illustrated in this section can be generalized (beyond pure factor analysis) to covariance structures. In particular, it is possible to combine the features of factor analysis with the features of path analysis or regression analysis. For example, if one has a set of variables representing indicators of a theoretical variable (F_1) that affect another theoretical variable (F_2) for which we also have a set of indicator variables, such a system of relationships can easily be analyzed by an extension of confirmatory factor analysis. In this particular example, the model can be specified as a confirmatory factor analysis with two correlated factors as shown in Figure 6. Also note that such a model is not different for the structure specified in Table 9 (sample 1), with no restriction on the correlation between factors. Here we have merely mentioned the most simple extension of confirmatory factor analysis; interested readers should consult Jöreskog (1970), and Sörbom and Jöreskog (1976) for a more complete presentation.

COMPARING FACTOR STRUCTURES

Another use of confirmatory factor analysis is comparing factor structures across several groups. For instance, one may hypothesize that the factor structure of political attitudes for blacks is the same as that of whites, or that the cognitive structure of one society is the same as that of another. It is also possible to specify that certain aspects of the factor structures are the same but others are dissimilar across the groups.

There exists a computer program (COFAMM: Confirmatory Factor Analysis with Model Modifications by Jöreskog and Sörbom) which can handle very general hypotheses. For instance, it allows all the variations that are available in testing factorial hypotheses for a single group—some parameters may be fixed or left to vary freely, or some parameters may be made to be constrained to be equal to the other parameters. In addition, with use of "constrained" parameters, any part of the parameter structure for one group can be made to be equal to that of another group.

As an illustration, consider the example of political attitudes where one is interested in comparing the factor structure of whites to that of blacks. The specific hypothesis may take the form: (1) there are two oblique factors for both whites and blacks, (2) the variables X_1 (money for schools), X_2 (money to reduce unemployment), and X_3 (control of big business) load on the same factor with the same loadings for both whites and blacks; likewise, X_4 (busing programs) and X_5 (job quotas) load on the other factor for both races, (3) but X_6 (headstart program) is expected to load differently for these two groups. In this case, one can specify the parameters for the whites as in a single group analysis and all the parameters for the blacks except one (involving X_6) as constrained to be the same as whites. Fairly extensive examples of confirmatory factor analysis as well as more general "covariance structure" analysis are available in Jöreskog (1976).

VI. CONSTRUCTION OF FACTOR SCALES

After examining factor analysis results, one may construct factor scales for two different reasons. First, having found some underlying dimensions in the data, the researcher may want to examine the cases in terms of these dimensions rather than in terms of each variable separately. Second, the researcher may want to use one or more factors as variables in another study. In fact, with the exception of the psychometric literature, factor analysis seems to have been used more often as a means of creating factor scales for other studies than as a means of studying factor structures per se. In this section, we will examine various procedures for creating factor scales. The methods to be examined are: (1) regression estimates, (2) estimates based on ideal-variables, or the "least squares" criterion, (3) Bartlett's method of minimizing the error variance, and (4) estimates with orthogonality constraints. In addition, we will examine (5) simple summation of variables with high factor loadings, and (6) creation of principal component scales. These methods will be discussed in the context of several important aspects of scaling.

Indeterminancy of Factor Scales

Initially, let us assume we have error-free data, and also that the data have been created by a known one-common factor model. The main objective of factor scale construction is to determine the value for each case on the common factor (F) on the basis of the observed variables, X's. Reflecting on material presented thus far, it should be obvious that it may not be possible to identify exactly the common factor from the variables because each variable also contains a unique component which is inseparably mixed with the common part of the variable. In general, the most one can do is obtain *estimates* of the values of common factors from the variables. For this reason, we say there is always some indeterminancy associated with creating factor scales.

To illustrate this, let us consider a one-common factor model with three variables. In particular, let us assume that all the factor loadings are the same (or that all the correlations have the same magnitude). Such an example is shown in the left half of Figure 7. Recall that given such a model, the observed correlations among variables are given by the multiplication of respective factor loadings, which in this case amounts to the square of one factor loading, because all the factor loadings are the same:

$$r_{ij} = b_i b_j = b_i^2 = b_j^2 = h^2. \qquad [39]$$

This equation also shows that an observed correlation is equivalent to the communality of the variable.

We can then construct an index (or factor scale if you prefer) by combining the observed Xs. Because each variable has the same loading on the common factor, it is reasonable in this case to give equal weight to each and add them. The resulting index is given by

$$\hat{F} = X_1 + X_2 + X_3,$$

with the causal operation depicted in the right half of Figure 7. Note in particular that the index $\hat{F}$ has four ultimate source variables—the common factor F and the three unique factors, U_1, U_2, and U_3. Therefore, because of the presence of unique factors, the correlation between F and $\hat{F}$ will not be perfect. We next will examine the degree of association between the underlying common factor and the factor scale, i.e., the reliability of the scale.

RELIABILITY OF A FACTOR SCALE

The variance of the scale ($\hat{F}$) is easily derivable by applying the algebra of expectations as used in Section II of the first volume. The resulting variance of $\hat{F}$, expressed in terms of variances of the Xs is:

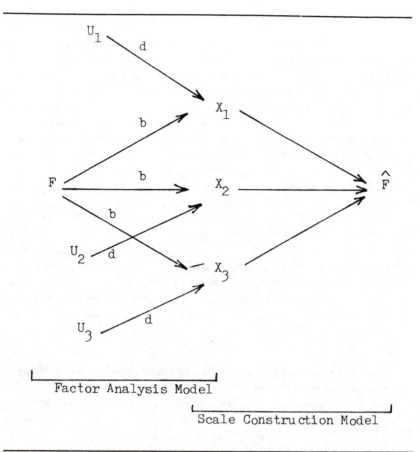

Figure 7: Path model illustrating relationship between factor and factor score

$$\text{var } (\hat{F}) = \text{var } (X_1) + \text{var } (X_2) + \text{var } (X_3) + \qquad [40]$$

$$2[\text{Cov}(X_1,X_2) + \text{Cov}(X_1,X_3) + \text{Cov}(X_2,X_3)].$$

The simplification is due to the weights being 1 in this example. This formula can be simplified further by noting that the variance of each variable is assumed to be 1, and the covariances are not only equal to the correlations but also to each other:

$$\text{Var } (\hat{F}) = n + 2[r_{12} + r_{13} + r_{23}] \qquad [41]$$

$$= n + n(n-1)r$$

(This is in fact no more than summing up all the entries in a correlation matrix of Xs.)

$$= n[1 + (n-1)r]$$

$$= n[1 + (n-1)h^2]$$

because, $r_{12} = r_{13} = r_{23} = r = h_i^2$ (see equation 39).

Some of the variance in $\hat{F}$ is, however, contributed by the unique factors, with their contribution being $\Sigma d_i^2 = \Sigma(1-h_i^2)$, which is further simplified to $n(1-h^2)$ because all the communalities are assumed equal in this example. Therefore, the portion of the variance $\hat{F}$ accounted for by the common factor F is simply

$$r^2_{(F,\hat{F})} = \frac{Var(\hat{F}) - n(1-h^2)}{var(\hat{F})}$$
$$= \frac{n[1+(n-1)h^2] - n(1-h^2)}{n[1+(n-1)h^2]}$$
$$= \frac{nh^2}{1+(n-1)h^2}$$
$$= \frac{nr}{1+(n-1)r} ,$$

[42]

which is equivalent to the Spearman-Brown formula for reliability, a special case of Cronbach's alpha (Cronbach, 1951; Lord and Novick, 1968). (You need to remember that, in this case, h^2 can be replaced by the correlation r.)

To familiarize the reader with the degree of indeterminancy or the degree of expected "reliability" of factor scales, we have presented in Table 11 "reliability" values for some typical combinations of communalities and number of variables. Note that as the number of variables increases for a fixed value of the communality (the factor loadings or the correlation), the reliability increases. Note also that even with fairly high uniform factor loadings (say .8), the reliability is relatively low if one has only a few variables to deal with.

We should also note that in constructing scales, one often standardizes $\hat{F}$ such that its mean = 0 and variance = 1. Such standardization is straightforward and can be incorporated into the weights, but its value is merely cosmetic.

TABLE 11
Expected Reliability (the Correlation Between the
Factor and Its Scale Squared) for Different Values of
Uniform Factor Loadings and Number of Variables[a]

Factor Loadings	.4	.5	.6	.7	.8	.9
Communality (h^2) or Correlation Between Variables	.16	.25	.36	.49	.64	.81
Number of Variables						
2	.276	.400	.529	.658	.780	.895
3	.364	.500	.628	.742	.842	.927
4	.432	.571	.692	.794	.877	.945
6	.533	.667	.771	.852	.914	.962
8	.604	.727	.818	.885	.934	.972
12	.696	.800	.871	.920	.955	.981
20	.792	.870	.918	.951	.973	.988

a. Formula for reliability $(\alpha) = \dfrac{n(r)}{1+(n-1)r} = \dfrac{n(h^2)}{1+(n-1)h^2}$

UNEQUAL FACTOR LOADINGS

Thus far we have assumed not only uniform factor loadings in a one-common factor model but also an error-free model. We will now examine what happens when we complicate the situation. Consider a stituation in which factor loadings in a one-common factor model are not all uniform. This will lead to a matrix of correlation coefficients with varying magnitudes. If one were to build a factor index by simply summing up the observed variables, the resulting scale would have a reliability given by:

$$\text{Cronbach's } a = \frac{\text{Sum of the elements in the reduced correlation matrix}}{\text{Sum of the elements in the correlation matrix}}$$

$$= \frac{\text{Var}(\hat{F}) - \Sigma\, d_i^2}{\text{Var}(\hat{F})} = \frac{\text{Var}(\hat{F}) - \Sigma(1-h_1^2)}{\text{Var}(\hat{F})} \quad [43]$$

This is equivalent to equation 42 if all the communalties are uniform. In general, given the same amount of average communality (or average correlation), the reliability will be greater when loadings are uniform than when they are not. Therefore, Table 11 gives a fairly good representation of the upper limit of the reliabilities for several sets of loadings which average those given in the table.

But the more crucial question is whether one should use equal weights in constructing the factor scale given different factor loadings. Let us consider an extreme case in which one of the communalities is 1—that is, an observed variable is coterminous with the underlying factor. In that case, one can describe the underlying factor by using that particular variable while ignoring all other variables; adding other variables with communalities less than 1 will simply contaminate the scale.

In general, then, it is not appropriate to simply sum *all* the variables to construct the factor scale when the factor loadings are not uniform. When the one-common factor model fits the data exactly, as is assumed here, the optimal solution is relatively simple; the weights to assign to each variable are obtained by

$$B' (R^{-1}) \qquad\qquad [44]$$

(where B is the vector of factor loadings and R is the correlation matrix for the Xs)

which is equivalent to regression weights obtained when the factor is regressed on the variables. Here the correlation between F and $\hat{F}$ will be maximized and its squared value is given by:

$$\text{Generalized Reliability} = \frac{\text{var}(\hat{F}) - \Sigma (1 - h_i^2) w_i^2}{\text{var}(\hat{F})} \qquad\qquad [45]$$

where w_i is the regression weight for each variable given by equation 44, and the total variance of the constructed scale is given by

$$\text{var}(\hat{F}) = \sum_i \sum_j w_i w_j r_{ij}, \qquad\qquad [46]$$

which is equivalent to summing up all the elements in the adjusted correlation matrix—where each element is multiplied by the two respective regression weights w_i and w_j. (The adjusted matrix will contain in its main diagonal squares of each weight for a given variable.) Since this value is equivalent to multiple R^2, it will be not less than the highest communality. Therefore, if one variable is an exact replica of the underlying common factor, that variable will get all the weight and other variables will be ignored.

An additional important point to remember in index construction is that when one uses differential weights, having a variable with a high loading is often more important than just having many variables with moderate loadings. Also keep in mind that the reliability of the scale will be at least as good as the square of the highest factor loading.

Sampling Variability and Different Criteria of Fit

So far we have dealt with an ideal situation in which a one factor model fits the data perfectly and there is no sampling variability. (Of course, this implies that we assume the underlying model is perfectly identified.) When sampling variability is introduced to the data, the relationships observed in the sample will not perfectly correspond to what is true in the population. Even if a one-common factor model fits the data perfectly in the population, such a model will not completely account for the sample correlations observed in the data This complication required that researchers adopt a criterion of fit between the scale and the underlying factor. There are three criteria proposed in the literature:

REGRESSION METHOD

The first criterion is to find a factor scale ($\hat{F}$) in such a way that the correlation between the underlying common factor (F) and the scale ($\hat{F}$) is maximum. Or differently stated, the criterion is to minimize the sum of the squared deviations between the two, that is, minimize $\Sigma(F-\hat{F})^2$. Meeting this criterion involves application of the regression solution. Such a solution is possible because factor analysis provides us with the factor loadings, which are equivalent to the correlations between the factor (to be predicted in scale construction) and the observed variables (to be used as predictors), and the correlations among the predictors which are no more than observed correlations among Xs. These two sets of correlations are all we need to solve the normal equations in regression. The predicted scores are given by

$$\hat{F} = XR^{-1}B, \qquad [47]$$

where B is the matrix of factor loadings, the Xs are the observed variables, and R is the correlation matrix for the Xs. Note that the weighting coefficients are those shown earlier (equation 44). The only difference is that in equation 47 we could have used the predicted correlations (BB′) in the place of the actual correlations without altering the principle, because in the error-free population model the two are equivalent. In the present context, the reproduced correlations will in general not be the same as the observed correlations. The expected reliability of the scale will be given by the same formula as equation 45.

LEAST SQUARES CRITERION

In the one-common factor model, each variable is considered as a weighted sum of common and unique factors:

$$X_j = b_j F + d_j u_j.$$

Next, consider inserting in the place of F the predicted $\hat{F}$ for the factor scale. The criterion is to construct $\hat{F}$ in such a way that the following sum of squares is minimum.

$$\text{Minimize} \quad \sum_i \sum_j (X_{ij} - b_j \hat{F}_j)^2. \quad [48]$$

Such a criterion leads to the weights given by

$$\hat{F} = X(BB')^{-1}B. \quad [49]$$

Note that the only important differences between this and equation 47 is that here we use the reproduced correlation (BB′) in the place of the observed correlations (R). Therefore, the two criteria would lead to the same index when one is dealing with population variables which fit the one-common factor model perfectly. However, the two diverge as sample correlations diverge from population correlations.

BARTLETT'S CRITERION

The third criterion involves examining the fit while taking the sampling variability into consideration. If we consider, as we did in maximum likelihood factoring, the unique variances as quasi-error variances, it makes sense to give less weight to the variables containing more random errors than the ones with fewer random errors. Hence, the criterion to use here is to minimize the sum of squares given in equation 48 after weighting each element with the reciprocals of the error variance. The criterion involves minimizing:

$$\sum_i \sum_j (X_{ij} - b_j \hat{F}_j)^2 / d_i^2. \quad [50]$$

The result is that variables with lower communalities are given less weight. Therefore, this criterion will not lead to the same scale as the preceding two whenever the factor loadings are not uniform. The formula (equation 51) for obtaining the factor scale looks formidable, but the underlying principle is not that incomprehensible:

$$\hat{F} = XU^{-2}B(B'U^{-2}B)^{-1},$$ [51]

where U^2 is the diagonal matrix of unique variances. The presence of U^{-2} may be considered as weighting in the manner described above.

Multiple Common Factors and Additional Complexities

Let us now complicate the situation even further, by assuming we have more than two-common factors. The three criteria discussed in the previous section are generalizable to the multivariate situation, and are generalizable to both orthogonal and oblique factor solutions. In addition, what we have discussed in relation to one-common factor is true in the multivariate case in relation to any specific common factor under consideration. However, the fact that the scales we create will not in general correlate perfectly with the respective underlying factors immediately raises two additional questions in the multifactor context: (1) will the imperfect scales be orthogonal to each other if the underlying factors are orthogonal; (2) will each scale correlate only with the factor it is supposed to measure and not with others (a factor scale is called *univocal* if its partial correlation with other underlying factors is zero after controlling for the factor it is a measure of)? In general these requirements are not simultaneously met by any scaling methods. The factor scales will be correlated among themselves even if the underlying factors are assumed to be orthogonal; also, the correlations among the factor scales will not correctly reflect the underlying correlations among the factors when the oblique factor model is assumed. Finally, a scale for one factor will be correlated with other underlying factors.

There is a special situation in which these requirements are met: (1) the factor analytic model fits the data exactly and there is no sampling or measurement error, and (2) each variable loads only on one factor. If these two conditions are met, one can consider each factor or dimension separately, and the situation reverts to the one-common factor model with error-free data as discussed earlier. We have noted that, under such conditions, there is no ambiguity as to the choice of scale construction—all the criteria we have examined lead to equivalent scales. Unfortunately, such an ideal situation is never found in practice.

There is, however, another situation in which the requirements of orthogonality and univocality of scales are met by some of the scaling methods. If the initial unrotated factors are obtained by means of the maximum likelihood (or canonical method), the factor scales for these unrotated factors would be both orthogonal and univocal if these scales are constructed by either the regression or the Bartlett method. This provides only partial consolation, however, because one is unlikely to expect the underlying factor model to be orthogonal. In addition, after orthogonal rotation, the regression method does not meet either of the requirements, whereas Barlett's method meets only the univocality requirement. None of the methods discussed so far lead to orthogonal scales.

These results provide some motivation for considering the fourth criterion introduced by Anderson and Rubin (1956). The Anderson-Rubin criterion is a modification of Bartlett's; it minimizes the weighted sums of squares used in Bartlett's criterion under the constraint that the created scales be orthogonal to each other. Consequently, regardless of whether the factors are rotated or not, as long as they are based on an orthogonal solution, this criterion produces factor scales that are uncorrelated to each other. However, the scales are not univocal for the rotated solution even if the initial solution is based on the maximum likelihood method.

THE CHOICE

In making a choice among these, the researcher must consider properties that are inherent in the method as well as extra-factor analytic ones. Below we offer some summary remarks about the inherent properties. First, in terms of correlations between the underlying factor and its respective scale, the regression method is superior to Bartlett's, but Bartlett's is superior to the least squares method. In terms of the univocality requirement, Bartlett's method fares best, but in terms of orthogonality requirement, the Anderson-Rubin criterion is preferable. However, assuming that in most research situations the researcher is unlikely to insist on the orthogonality of underlying factors, the real choice seems to be between the regression method and Bartlett's method.

Several additional considerations, some of which complicate the choice and some of which simplify it, should be discussed. First, there is usually a very high correlation among the scales produced by different scaling methods; hence, for many research problems the choice may be academic. One type of scale construction can serve as well as the other (see Horn, 1965; Alwin, 1973). Second, the choice is also dependent upon the specific research problem at hand. Tucker (1971) notes that when factor scales are to be related to outside variables, some methods are better for particular types of analysis. More specifically, he demonstrates that the scales produced by the regression method do not allow one to correctly estimate the underlying correlations between the hypothesized factors and the outside variables, whereas others may allow such estimation. On the other hand, if the major purpose of using factor scales is to use them as predictors of outside variables, the scales based on the regression method are better.

Keep in mind, however, that the discussion so far has been based on the assumption that the factor model fits the data exactly in the population, and thus, any discrepancy between the model and data is assumed to be the result of random sampling error. What happens, however, if such an exact fit is not expected, or if the factor analysis is used only as a heuristic means of sorting out major clusters of variables in the data? Under such circumstances, all of the finer points we have examined may become minor issues in comparison to the extra-factor analytic considerations.

Factor-based Scales

There are two completely different reasons for which one may consider creating *scales utilizing only some of the information* obtained from factor analysis instead of relying on factor scales we have discussed so far. First, one may accept the proposition that the factor analytic model fits the data exactly in the population, but assume that some of the particular values obtained in a factor solution are subject to sampling errors. Here one may ignore specific variations in the factor loadings and consider only one type of information as relevant: either a variable loads on a given factor or it does not. Consequently, a scale is built by summing all the variables with substantial loadings and ignoring the remaining variables with minor loadings. The scale created in this way is no longer a factor scale but merely factor-based. The specific reasons behind such a scale construction are that (1) even if factor loadings are zero for some variables in the population, they will not be zero in a specific sample solution; (2) even if the factor loadings are uniform in the population, they will not be so in a sample. The rule of thumb often used in this context is to consider factor loadings less than .3 as not substantial.

Whether this type of scale construction is justifiable or not depends on the degree to which the specific assumptions underlying it are appropriate. Ideally, one should test these assumptions through the use of confirmatory factor analysis. However, if such a "simple loading pattern" is supported by confirmatory analysis, it is no longer a factor-based scale but a legitimate factor scale. In practice, however, even if such tests were

TABLE 12
Results of Confirmatory Factor Analysis, Using Correlation
Matrix from the Upper Triangle of Table 1 and the
Model Specified in Table 7*

| Variables | Factors | | Communality |
	F_1	F_2	h^2
X_1	.792	0	.624
X_2	.756	0	.571
X_3	.633	0	.501
X_4	0	.577	.333
X_5	0	.669	.448
X_6	0	.635	.404

$$r_{F_1F_2} = .501$$

$\chi^2 = 4.6534$
df = 8
probability = .7939

*These results are obtained from LISREL III, not from COFAMM.

made and they show statistically significant deviations, it is a matter of degree and minor deviations from the simple loadings can still be ignored for the reasons to be given below.

There is a completely different basis for justifying the practice of simple index construction. (We are taking for granted that this type of scaling is the simplest, but this is not the strongest reason for using it.) Often the factor analytic model is not expected to fit the data completely for several reasons: (1) non-random measurement errors in the variables, and (2) minor factors unspecified and conceptually unrelated to the domain of interest, may account for some correlations observed, and these in turn affect the weights obtained. Therefore, there is a basis for not taking the specific values obtained in a given factor solution at face value. The conservative stance is to view the structures found by the factor analysis as only suggestive, indicating some clustering in the data but no more. Put another way, once we accept that the particular numbers obtained contain substantial "noise," it may be wise to ignore minor distinctions and differences.

It is likely that some will object to the cavalier attitude taken in this type of scale construction. One might be concerned with the fact that the combination of observed variables is not optimal in the sense that some differential weighting can increase the overall correlation between the scale and the observed variables. (That is, the concern is with the efficiency of simple summing as a means of representing information contained in raw variables.) Even on this point, simple weighting can be justified because the multiple correlation between the scale (some combination of variables) and the total set of variables does not change very much for minor variation in the weighting (Wang and Stanley, 1970; Wainer, 1976). One caution, as mentioned in Section III, should be noted. If the factor analytic solution is believed to be faithful to the data, ignoring very high factor loadings—say above .9—and giving them the same weight as the item with a low loading is counter-productive. In summary, we are arguing that both factor scales and factor-based scales have a legitimate place in practical research.

Component Scores

Finally, we would like to comment on scales based on principal components analysis. As noted earlier (rather emphatically), the underlying principle of principal components analysis is different from that of factor analysis. Therefore, one cannot be used as a substitute for the other. But in a larger context of practical research, both have legitimate uses. There are situations in which the component scores may be preferred to the factor scales. In particular, if the objective is some simple summary of information contained in the raw data without recourse to factor analytic assumptions, the use of component scores has a definite advantage over factor scaling. This is why it is important, at least briefly, to comment on component scales.

As noted earlier, the principal components are no more than exact mathematical transformations of the raw variables. Therefore, it is possible to represent the components exactly from the combination of raw variables, and we can speak of component *scores,* instead of *scales* or *estimates.* The scores are obtained by combining the raw variables with weights that are proportional to their component (factor) loadings.

$$\text{Component Score} = \sum_{j} [(b_{ij}/\lambda_i)X_j], \qquad [52]$$

where b_{ij} is the component loading for the jth variable on i^{th} component, and λ_i is the associated eigenvalue. The division by the eigenvalue is cosmetic in that it merely assures that the resulting index has a variance equal to 1.

NOTE

1. When the underlying structure is complex, as in Thurstone's box problem, it is often difficult to recover exactly the underlying pattern from the covariance matrix purely on the basis of some analytical criteria. One may need the aid of fitting hyperplanes and visual rotations.

VII. BRIEF ANSWERS TO QUESTIONS FREQUENTLY ASKED

Questions Pertaining to the Nature of Variables and Their Measurement

(a) *What level of measurement is required for factor analysis?*

Factor analysis requires that the variables be measured at least at the interval level (Stevens, 1946). This requirement is implied by the use of correlation or covariance matrices as the basic input to factor analysis. In addition, the specification of variables as the weighted sum of the underlying factors and the construction of factor scales as a weighted sum of the observed variables is not clearly defined for ordinal or nominal variables.

(b) *Is it appropriate to use measures of association such as Kendall's tau, and Goodman and Kruskal's gamma in place of ordinary correlations?*

The answer is no. As noted above, the operation of addition is not well defined for ordinal variables and, therefore, there is no factor analytic model that incorporates ordinal variables. One may use such a matrix in factor analysis for purely heuristic purposes, but the statistical interpretation to be given to the results is not well defined. (There are some nonmetric scaling methods developed specifically to deal with nonmetric variables.)

(c) *Based on the above answers, must a researcher always avoid using factor analysis when the metric base for the variables is not clearly established?*

Not necessarily. Many variables, such as measures of attitudes and opinions and numerous kinds of items for testing achievement do not have a clearly established metric base. However, it is generally assumed that many "ordinal variables" may be given numeric values without distorting the underlying properties. The final answer to this question really hinges on two considerations: (1) how well the arbitrarily assigned numbers reflect the underlying true distances, and (2) the amount of distortion introduced in the correlations (which become the basic input to factor analysis) by the distortions in the scaling. Fortunately, the correlation coefficients are fairly robust with respect to ordinal distortions in the measurement (Labovitz, 1967, 1970; Kim, 1975). Hence, as long as one can assume that the distortions introduced by assigning numeric values to ordinal categories are believed to be *not* very substantial, treating ordinal variables as if they are metric variables can be justified. Nevertheless, one should be aware of possible distortions, even if minor, in the factor analytic results owing to nonrandom measurement errors.

(d) *What about dichotomous variables? There are people who believe it is okay to use factor analysis on dichotomous variables (1) because assigning numbers to a dichotomy does not really require measurement assumptions, and (2) because, as a result, the phi (ϕ) is equivalent to the Pearson correlation coefficient, which is the appropriate measure of association for factor analysis. Therefore, isn't it appropriate to apply factor analysis to the matrix of phi's?*

The answer is no. For one thing, one cannot express the dichotomous variables within the factor analytic model. To be more specific, recall from Kim/ Mueller, University Paper 07-013, Section II, that in factor analysis each variable is assumed to be a weighted sum of at least two underlying factors (one common and one unique). Even if these underlying factors have two values as shown in Table 1 of University Paper 07-013 (which is a very unlikely occurrence in real factor models), the resulting values in the observed variable must contain at least four different values, which clearly is inconsistent with a dichotomous variable. Therefore, nothing can justify the use of factor analysis on dichotomous data except a purely heuristic set of criteria. The following three questions are also relevant.

(e) *But the implications of the preceding answer are quite disturbing. Because we normally conceive of our underlying factors as potentially continuous, we should expect our variables to contain numerous categories. However, most of the variables we deal with usually have a very limited number of categories—yes or no; agree or disagree; at best, strongly agree, agree, neutral, disagree, strongly disagree, etc. Does this really mean we are applying factor analysis to data that are inconsistent with factor analysis models?*

In a sense, yes. The variables with limited categories are in a strict sense not compatible with factor analytic models. If one considers that the observed variables represent the crude measurement or grouping of adjacent values, the question is no longer whether the data are intrinsically incompatible with the factor analysis model but whether and how much the nonrandom measurement errors distort the factor analytic results. Grouping of values certainly affects the correlations, but the extent of this will depend on the degree of coarseness of grouping, the shape of the distribution, and so on. There are, however, some encouraging comments about the use of factor analysis as a heuristic device even under severe measurement distortions (see the next question).

(f) *Under what circumstances can one use factor analysis on data containing dichotomies or variables with a limited number of categories?*

In general the greater the number of categories, the smaller the degree of distortion. Even in dichotomies, the use of phi's can be justified if factor analysis is used as a means of finding general clusterings of variables, and if the underlying correlations among variables are believed to be moderate—say less than .6 or .7. The reason is that dichotomization of continuous variables attenuates the correlations and the attenuation is also affected by the cutting points. However, when the underlying correlations are not very high, the effects of varying cutting points on correlations are negligible. Therefore, the grouping attenuates correlations in general but does not affect the structure of clustering in the data—this is because factor analysis is dependent on the relative magnitude of correlations. If the researcher's goal is to search for clustering patterns, the use of factor analysis may be justified (see Kim, Nie and Verba (1977) for an illustration).

(g) *If the distortion due to the cutting point is more critical than the overall attentuation due to grouping, why not use adjustments such as using ϕ/ϕ_{max} or R/R_{max} in the place of ϕ or r?*

This correction is appropriate only when the underlying distributional shape takes a particular (very unlikely) form (see Carrol, 1961), or when the underlying correlations among the continuous variables are perfect. If the correlations are perfect, there is no point in performing factor analysis. Hence, the use of such a correction is contradictory (see Kim et al., 1977).

(h) *Aren't there some methods that can handle these measurement problems more directly?*

There are two approaches suggested in the literature. Both of these approaches assume that the dichotomous or polychotomous variables are results of some grouping or threshold effects, and these variables are indicators of underlying continuous variables for which the factor analysis models exactly apply. Consequently, in order to solve for the factor structure one has to find out the correlations among the *underlying* variables. One way of doing this is to use tetrachoric correlations instead of phi's. This approach is only heuristic because the calculation of tetrachorics can often break down and the correlation matrix may not be Gramian (see Bock and Lieberman, 1970). Another approach is to directly deal with the underlying multivariate distribution instead of calculating tetrachorics on the basis of bivariate tables. This is a promising line of attack, but currently the computing is expensive even with modern computers (see Christoffersson, 1975).

Questions Pertaining to the Use of Correlation or Covariance Matrices

(a) *Does it make any difference whether one uses the covariance matrix or the correlation matrix?*

It depends on (1) whether the variables have comparable metrics, (2) what type of extraction method is used, and (3) whether or not one is comparing one factor structure to another. If one is considering only one group (or sample) and is using a scale-free extraction method such as the maximum likelihood solution, Alpha factoring, or image analysis, it does not make any difference whether one uses one type of matrix or the other, *when the objective is to identify relevant underlying dimensions*. If the covariance matrix is used and scales vary widely, scale factors will complicate interpretation of the results, however. It is, therefore, advisable to use a correlation matrix if the variances differ from variable to variable and the scales vary substantially (as would be the case if one variable is measured in dollars, another in years or schooling, and a third on a 5-point Likert scale). Furthermore, the use of the correlation matrix is recommended on practical grounds; some computer programs do not accept a covariance matrix, and most examples in the literature are based on correlation matrices.

(b) *When is the use of the covariance matrix preferable then?*

The covariance matrix is preferable when comparison of factors structures between groups are contemplated. The reason is that the correlation matrix is obtained by scaling variables according to sample-specific standards—such as sample means and variances. For this reason, even theoretically invariant parameters involved in factor analysis cannot be expected to be invariant from group to group (or sample to sample) because the measurement scales are restandardized from group to group when the correlations are computed. (See Kim and Mueller (1979) for an expository discussion of the implications of standardizing variables in causal analysis in general; also, Sörbom and Jöreskog, 1976:90.)

(c) *What should be done if the objective is to compare factor structures across the groups when the variables are measured on widely different scales?*

One strategy is to standardize the variables, using a common standard such as the mean and variance of the combined group as a reference group. Then the variance-covariance matrix for each group could be calculated. This is different from using group specific correlation matrices, which implies transforming variables in each group using group (or sample) specific standards.

Questions Pertaining to Significance Tests and Stability of Factor Solution

(a) *When the maximum likelihood solution and associated significance test are used, what is the minimum sample size required?*

The greater the sample size, the better the χ^2 approximation. Lawley and Maxwell (1971) suggest that the test is appropriate if the sample contains at least 51 more cases than the number of variables under consideration. That is, $N - n - 1 \geq 50$, where N is the sample size and n is the number of variables. This is, of course, only a general rule-of-thumb.

(b) *How many variables should one have for each hypothesized factor?*

Thurstone suggests at least three variables for each factor, but this requirement need not be met if confirmatory factory analysis is used. In general, researchers seem to agree that one should have at least twice as many variables as factors. For the minimum number of variables for significance testing, see Table 20 in Section III.

(c) *Is the assumption that variables are multivariate normal always necessary?*

The factor analysis model itself does not require such an assumption. For example, it is possible to build a factor analytic model even using dichotomous factors. However, the maximum likelihood solution and the associated significance test require the assumption. In general, however, the consequences of violating this assumption are not clearly understood.

Other Miscellaneous Statistical Questions

(a) *What is the meaning of the signs of the factor loadings?*

The sign itself has no intrinsic meaning, and in no way should it be used to assess the magnitude of the relationship between the variable and the factor. However, signs for variables for a given factor have a specific meaning relative to the signs for other variables; the different signs simply mean that the variables are related to that factor in opposite directions. For this reason, it is advisable to code the variables in the same direction before factor analyzing them.

(b) *What is the meaning of the eigenvalues associated with rotated factors? What is the relevance of the proportion of variance explained by a given rotated factor?*

The eigenvalues associated with unrotated factors do not have the same meaning given the eigenvalues for rotated factors, with the exception that the eigenvalue sums are the same. In initial factoring, the magnitude of descending values of eigenvalues tells us something about the relative importance of each factor. This is not true for the rotated solution. Once different dimensions are separated out through rotation, it is not crucial to know how much variance in the data as a whole each explains.

(c) *Is it appropriate to factor analyze using the relationships among the factor scales in order to obtain a "higher-order" factor solution?*

No. The correlations among the factor scales are not the same as the correlations among the underlying factors. One should use as the correlation matrix input to the higher-order factoring the correlation matrix produced by the oblique factor solution.

(d) *Can one claim that the underlying factor structure is orthogonal when such a solution is compatible with the data?*

No. Orthogonality is imposed by the researcher. However, if one finds an orthogonal structure when oblique rotations are applied, or if graphical representations show that variable clusterings form right angles, then one can claim that the underlying structure is orthogonal.

(e) *Can one include variables, some of which are causes of others? That is, is it necessary that all the variables be at the same level in the causal ordering?*

In general, the variables should not be causes of each other. The factor model assumes that all the observed variables are caused by the underlying factors. However, an experienced user may apply factor analysis to causal systems of variables for other purposes (see Stinchcombe, 1971).

Questions Pertaining to Books, Journals, and Computer Programs

(a) *Are there any books or articles on factor analysis a novice can read and readily understand?*

Not really. Most require some technical background. However, the following are easier than the others: Rummel (1967); Schuessler (1971); Cattell (1952); Comrey (1973); Fruchter (1954).

(b) *What are the "next-level" books that the serious reader should consider examining?*

Harman (1976); Mulaik (1972); Lawley and Maxwell (1971).

(c) *What are the major journals which regularly publish articles on factor analysis?*

Psychometrika; British Journal of Mathematical and Statistical Psychology; Educational and Psychological Measurement.

(d) *What are some of the general purpose computer packages containing factor analysis programs?*

SPSS; OSIRIS; SAS; BMD.

(e) What are the more specialized programs dealing with factor analysis one should know about?

Kaiser's—Little Jiffy, Mark IV; Sörbom and Jöreskog, COFAMM.

(f) *Where are the major simulation studies reported?*

Tucker, Koopman and Linn (1969); Browne (1968); Linn (1968); Hakstian (1971); Hakstian and Abell (1974).

REFERENCES

ALWIN, D. F. (1973) "The use of factor analysis in the construction of linear composites in social research." Sociological Methods and Research 2:191-214.

ANDERSON, T. W. and H. RUBIN (1956) "Statistical inference in factor analysis." Proceedings of the Third Berkeley Symposium on Mathematical Statistics and Probability 5:111-150.

ASHER, H. (1976) Causal Modeling. Sage University Papers on Quantitative Applications in the Social Sciences, 07-003. Beverly Hills and London: Sage Pub.

BMDP-77: Biomedical Computer Programs (P-Series). W. J. Dixon, Series Editor, M. B. Brown, Editor 1977 edition. Los Angeles: Univ. of California Press, 1977.

BARGMANN, R. E. (1957) A Study of Independence and Dependence in Multivariate Normal Analysis. Mimeo Series No. 186. Chapel Hill, N.C.: Institute of Statistics.

BARTLETT, M. S. (1937) "The statistical conception of method factors." British Journal of Psychology 28:97-104.

BOCK, R. D. and R. E. BARGMANN (1966) "Analysis of covariance structure." Psychometrika 31:507-534.

BOCK, R. D. and M. LIEBERMAN (1970) "Fitting a response model for N dichotomously scored items." Psychometrika 26:347-372.

BOCK, R. D. and A. C. PETERSON (1975) "A multivariate correction for attenuation." Biometrika 62:673-678.

BROWNE, M. W. (1968) "A comparison of factor analytic techniques." Psychometrika 33:267-334.

COFAMM: Confirmatory Factory Analysis with Model Modification User's Guide. Sörbom, D. and Jöreskog, K. G. Chicago: National Educational Resources, Inc., 1976.

CARROLL, J. B. (1953) "Approximating simple structure in factor analysis." Psychometrika 18:23-38.

———— (1961) "The nature of data, or how to choose a correlation coefficient." Psychometrika 26:347-372.

CATTELL, R. B. (1952) Factor Analysis. New York: Harper and Bros.

———— (1965) "Factor analysis: an introduction to essentials. (I) the purpose and underlying models, (II) the role of factor analysis in research." Biometrics 21:190-215, 405-435.

———— (1966) Handbook of Multivariate Experimental Psychology. Chicago: Rand McNally.

———— and J. L. MUERLE (1960) "The 'maxplane' program for factor rotation to oblique simple structure." Educational and Psychological Measurement 20:269-290.

CHRISTOFFERSSON, A. (1975) "Factor analysis of dichotomized variables." Psychometrika 40:5-32.

COMREY, A. L. (1973) A First Course in Factor Analysis. New York: Academic Press.

CRONBACH, L. J. (1951) "Coefficient alpha and the internal structure of tests." Psychometrika 16: 297-334.

DUNCAN, O. D. (1966) "Path analysis: sociological examples." American Journal of Sociology 72:1-16.

EBER, H. W. (1966) "Toward oblique simple structure maxplane." Multivariate Behavioral Research 1:112-125.

FRUCHTER, B. (1954) Introduction to Factor Analysis. New York: Van Nostrand.

GREEN, B. F., Jr. (1976) "On the factor score controversy." Psychometrika 41:263-266.

GUILFORD, J. P. (1977) "The invariance problem in factor analysis." Educational and Psychological Measurement 37:11-19.

GUTTMAN, L. (1953) "Image theory for the structure of quantitative variates." Psychometrika 18:227-296.

———— (1954) "Some necessary conditions for common factor analysis." Psychometrika 19:149-161.

HAKSTIAN, A. R. (1971) "A comparative evaluation of several prominent methods of oblique factor transformation." Psychometrika 36:175-193.

—— and R. A. ABELL (1974) "A further comparison of oblique factor transformation methods." Psychometrika 39:429-444.

HARMAN, H. H. (1976) Modern Factor Analysis. Chicago: University of Chicago Press.

—— (in press) "Minres method of factor analysis," in K. Enstein, A. Ralston, and H. S. Wilf (eds.) Statistical Methods for Digital Computers. New York: John Wiley.

—— and W. H. JONES (1966) "Factor analysis by minimizing residuals (Minres)." Psychometrika 31:351-368.

HARMAN, H. H. and Y. FUKUDA (1966) "Resolution of the Heywood case in the Minres solution." Psychometrika 31:563-571.

HARRIS, C. W. (1962) "Some Rao-Guttman relationships." Psychometrika 27: 247-263.

—— (1967) "On factors and factor scores." Psychometrika 32: 363-379.

—— and H. F. KAISER (1964) "Oblique factor analytic solutions by orthogonal transformations." Psychometrika 29:347-362.

HENDRICKSON, A. E. and P. O. WHITE (1964) "Promax: A quick method for rotation to oblique simple structure." British Journal of Mathematical and Statistical Psychology 17:65-70.

HORN, J. L. (1965) "An empirical comparison of various methods for estimating common factor scores." Educational and Psychological Measurement 25:313-322.

HORST, P. (1965) Factor Analysis of Data Matrices. New York: Holt Rinehart and Winston.

HOTELLING, H. (1933) "Analysis of a complex of statistical variables into principal components." Journal of Education Psychology 24:417-441, 498-520.

HOWE, W. G. (1955) Some Contributions to Factor Analysis. Report No. ORNL-1919. Oak Ridge, Tenn.: Oak Ridge National Laboratory. Ph.D. dissertation, University of North Carolina.

JENNRICH, R. I. (1970) "Orthogonal Rotation Algorithms." Psychometrika 35:229-235.

—— (1974) "Simplified formulae in standard errors in maximum likelihood factor analysis." British Journal of Mathematical and Statistical Psychology 27:122-131.

JENNRICH, R. I. and P. F. SAMPSON (1966) "Rotation for simple loadings." Psychometrika 31:313-323.

JÖRESKOG, K. G. (1963) Statistical Estimation in Factor Analysis: A New Technique and Its Foundation. Stockholm: Almquist and Wiksell.

—— (1966) "Testing a simple structure hypothesis in factor analysis." Psychometrika 31:165-178.

—— (1967) "Some contributions to maximum likelihood factor analysis." Psychometrika 32:443-482.

—— (1969) "A general approach to confirmatory maximum likelihood factor analysis." Psychometrika 34:183-202.

—— (1970) "A general method for analysis of covariance structure." Biometrika 57:239-251.

—— (1976) Analyzing Psychological Data by Structural Analysis of Covariance Matrices. Research Report 76-9. University of Uppsala, Statistics Department.

JÖRESKOG, K. G. and D. N. LAWLEY (1968) "New methods in maximum likelihood factor analysis." British Journal of Mathematical and Statistical Psychology 21:85-96.

KAISER, H. F. (1958) "The varimax criterion for analytic rotation in factor analysis." Psychometrika 23:187-200.

—— (1963) "Image analysis," pp. 156-166 in C. W. Harris (ed.) Problems in Measuring Change. Madison: University of Wisconsin Press.

—— (1970) "A second-generation Little Jiffy." Psychometrika 35:401-415.

—— (1974) "Little Jiffy, Mark IV." Educational and Psychological Measurement 34: 111-117.

—— (1974) "An index of factorial simplicity." Psychometrika 39:31-36.

KAISER, H. F. and J. CAFFREY (1965) "Alpha factor analysis." Psychometrika 30:1-14.

KIM, J. O. (1975) "Multivariate analysis of ordinal variables." American Journal of Sociology 81:261-298.

—— and C. W. MUELLER (1976) "Standardized and unstandardized coefficients in causal analysis: An expository note." Sociological Methods and Research 4:423-438.

KIM, J. O., N. NIE and S. VERBA (1977) "A note on factor analyzing dichotomous variables: the case of political participation." Political Methodology 4:39-62.

KIRK, D. B. (1973) "On the numerical approximation of the bivariate normal (tetrachoric) correlation coefficient." Psychometrika 38:259-268.

LISREL III: Estimation of Linear Structural Equation Systems by Maximum Likelihood Methods. (User's Guide). Jóreskog, K. G. and Sörbom, D. Chicago: National Educational Resources, Inc., 1976.

LITTLE JIFFY, MARK IV. (See Kaiser, 1974)

LABOVITZ, S. (1967) "Some observations on measurement and statistics." Social Forces 46:151-160.

—— (1970) "The assignment of numbers to rank order categories." American Sociological Review 35:515-524.

LAND, K. O. (1969) "Principles of path analysis," pp. 3-37 in E. F. Borgatta (ed.) Sociological Methodology. San Francisco: Jossey-Bass.

LAWLEY, D. N. (1940) "The estimation of factor loading by the method of maximum likelihood." Proceedings of the Royal Society of Edinburgh 60:64-82.

—— and MAXWELL, A. E. (1971) Factor Analysis as a Statistical Method. London: Butterworth and Co.

LEVINE, M. S. (1977) Canonical Analysis and Factor Comparison. Sage University Papers on Quantitative Applications in the Social Sciences, 07-006. Beverly Hills and London: Sage Pub.

LI, C. C. (1975) Path Analysis—A Primer. Pacific Grove, Calif.: Boxwood Press.

LINN, R. L. (1968) "A Monte Carlo approach to the number of factors problems." Psychometrika 33:37-71.

LORD, F. M. and W. R. NOVICK (1968) Statistical Theories of Mental Test Scores. Reading, Mass.: Addison-Wesley.

MALINVAND, E. (1970) Statistical Methods of Econometrics. New York: Elsevier.

MAXWELL, A. E. (1972) "Thomson's sampling theory recalled." British Journal of Mathematical and Statistical Psychology 25:1-21.

McDONALD, R. P. (1970) "The theoretical foundations of principal factor analysis, canonical factor analysis, and alpha factor analysis." British Journal of Mathematical and Statistical Psychology 23:1-21.

—— (1974) "The measurement of factor indeterminacy." Psychometrika 39:203-221.

—— (1975) "Descriptive axioms for common factor theory, image theory and component theory." Psychometrika 40:137-152.

—— (1975) "A note on Rippe's test of significance in common factor analysis." Psychometrika 40:117-119.

—— and E. J. BURR (1967) "A comparison of four methods of constructing factor scores." Psychometrika 32:380-401.

MULAIK, S. A. (1972) The Foundations of Factor Analysis. New York: McGraw-Hill.

NEUHAUS, J. O. and C. WRIGLEY (1954) "The method: an analytic approach to orthogonal simple structure." British Journal of Mathematical and Statistical Psychology 7:81-91.

OSIRIS Manual. Ann Arbor, Mich.: Inter-University Consortium for Political Research, 1973.

RAO, C. R. (1955) "Estimation and test of significance in factor analysis." Psychometrika 20:93-111.

RUMMEL, R. J. (1967) "Understanding factor analysis." Conflict Resolution 11:444-480.
——— (1970) Applied Factor Analysis. Evanston: Northwestern University Press.
SAS: A User's Guide to SAS 76. Anthony J. Barr, James H. Goodnight, John P. Sall, and Jane T. Helwig. Raleigh, N.C.: SAS Institute, Inc., 1976.
SPSS: Statistical Package for the Social Sciences. Norman H. Nie, C. Hadlai Hull, Jean G. Jenkins, Karin Steinbrenner, and Dale Bent. New York: McGraw-Hill, 1975.
SAUNDERS, D. R. (1953) An Analytic Method for Rotation to Orthogonal Simple Structure. Research Bulletin 53-10. Princeton, N.J.: Educational Testing Service.
——— (1960) "A computer program to find the best-fitting orthogonal factors for a given hypothesis." Psychometrika 25:199-205.
SCHUESSLER, K. (1971) Analyzing Social Data. Boston: Houghton Mifflin.
SÖRBOM, D. and K. G. JÖRESKOG (1976) COFAMM: Confirmatory Factor Analysis with Model Modification User's Guide. Chicago: National Educational Resources, Inc.
STEPHENSON, W. (1953) The Study of Behavior. Chicago: The University of Chicago Press.
STEVENS, S. S. (1946) "On the theory of scales of measurement." Science 103:677-680.
STINCHCOMBE, A. L. (1971) "A heuristic procedure for interpreting factor analysis." American Sociological Review 36:1080-1084.
THOMPSON, G. H. (1934) "Hotelling's method modified to give Spearman's g." Journal of Educational Psychology 25:366-374.
THURSTONE, L. L. (1947) Multiple Factor Analysis. Chicago: University of Chicago Press.
TRYON, C. R. and BAILEY, D. E. (1970) Cluster Analysis. New York: McGraw-Hill.
TUCKER, L. R. (1966) "Some mathematical notes on three mode factor analysis." Psychometrika 31:279-311.
——— (1971) "Relations of factor score estimates to their use." Psychometrika 36:427-436.
———, R. F. KOOPMAN, and R. L. LINN (1969) "Evaluation of factor analytic research procedures by means of simulated correlation matrices." Psychometrika 34:421-459.
TUCKER, L. R. and C. LEWIS (1973) "A reliability coefficient for maximum likelihood factor analysis." Psychometrika 38:1-8.
VELICER, W. F. (1975) "The relation between factor scores, image scores, and principal component scores." Educational and Psychological Measurement 36:149-159.
WAINER, H. (1976) "Estimating coefficients in linear models: it don't make no nevermind." Psychological Bulletin 83:213-217.
WANG, M. W. and J. C. STANLEY (1970) "Differential weighing: a review of methods and empirical studies." Review of Educational Research 40:663-705.

GLOSSARY

ALPHA FACTORING: a method of initial factoring in which the variables included in the analysis are considered samples from a universe of variables; see Kaiser and Caffrey in the references.

ADJUSTED CORRELATION MATRIX: the correlation matrix in which the diagonal elements are replaced by communalities; also used to refer to correlation or covariance matrices which are altered in a variety of ways before extracting factors.

BIQUARTIMIN CRITERION: a criterion applied in obtaining an indirect oblique rotation.

COMMUNALITY (h^2): the variance of an observed variable accounted for by the common factors; in an orthogonal factor model, it is equivalent to the sum of the squared factor loadings.

COMMON PART: that part of an observed variable accounted for by the common factors.

COMMON FACTOR: unmeasured (or hypothetical) underlying variable which is the source of variation in at least two observed variables under consideration.

CONFIRMATORY FACTOR ANALYSIS: factor analysis in which specific expectations concerning the number of factors and their loadings are tested on sample data.

CORRELATION: a measure of association between two variables; generally assumed to be the product-moment r (or Pearson's r); equivalent to the covariance between two standardized variables; also used as a general term for any type of linear association between variables.

COVARIATION: a crude measure of the degree to which two variables co-vary together; measured as the sum of cross-products of two variables which are expressed as deviations from their respective means; also used as a general term for describing the association between variables.

COVARIANCE: a measure of association between two variables; covariation divided by the number of cases involved; expected value of the sum of cross-products between two variables expressed as deviations from their respective means; the covariance between standardized variables is also known as the correlation.

COVARIANCE-STRUCTURE ANALYSIS: an analysis strategy (1) in which the observed covariance is expressed in terms of a very general model which can accommodate hypothetical factors as well as observed variables, and (2) in which the researcher then specifies appropriate parameters to evaluate the adequacy of the specification against the sample covariance structure.

COVARIMIN: a criterion for obtaining an oblique rotation; a variant of indirect oblimin rotation.

DETERMINANT: a mathematical property of a square matrix; discussed as a means of determining the rank (or the number of independent dimensions) of an adjusted correlation matrix.

DIRECT OBLIMIN: a method of oblique rotation in which rotation is performed without resorting to reference axes.

EIGENVALUE (or characteristic root): a mathematical property of a matrix; used in relation to the decomposition of a covariance matrix, both as a criterion of determining the number of factors to extract and a measure of variance accounted for by a given dimension.

EIGENVECTOR: a vector associated with its respective eigenvalue; obtained in the process of initial factoring; when these vectors are appropriately standardized, they become factor loadings.

EQUIMAX: a criterion for obtaining an orthogonal rotation; this criterion is a compromise between varimax and quartimax criteria.

ERROR-FREE DATA: contrived data where the underlying model is presumed known and there is an exact fit between data and model.

EXPECTATION: a mathematical operation through which the mean of a random variable is defined for both discrete and continuous distributions; an expected value is the property of a particular variable.

EXPLORATORY FACTOR ANALYSIS: factor analysis which is mainly used as a means of exploring the underlying factor structure *without* prior specification of number of factors and their loadings.

EXTRACTION OF FACTORS OR FACTOR EXTRACTION: the initial stage of factor analysis in which the covariance matrix is resolved into a smaller number of underlying factors or components.

ERROR COMPONENT: the part of the variance of an observed variable that is due to random measurement errors; constitutes a portion of the unique component.

FACTORS: hypothesized, unmeasured, and underlying variables which are presumed to be the sources of the observed variables; often divided into unique and common factors.

FACTOR LOADING: a general term referring to a coefficient in a factor pattern or structure matrix.

FACTOR PATTERN MATRIX: a matrix of coefficients where the columns usually refer to common factors and the rows to the observed variables; elements of the matrix represent regression weights for the common factors where an observed variable is assumed to be a linear combination of the factors; for an orthogonal solution, the pattern matrix is equivalent to correlations between factors and variables.

FACTOR SCORE: the estimate for a case on an underlying factor formed from a linear combination of observed variables; a by-product of the factor analysis.

FACTOR STRUCTURE MATRIX: a matrix of coefficients where the coefficients refer to the correlations between factors and variables; it is equivalent to a pattern matrix in the orthogonal case.

FACTORICAL COMPLEXITY: a characteristic of an observed variable; the number of common factors with (significant) loadings on that variable.

FACTORIAL DETERMINATION: the overall degree to which variations in observed variables are accounted by the common factors.

GRAMIAN: a square matrix is Gramian if it is symmetrical and all of the eigenvalues associated with the matrix are greater than or equal to zero; unadjusted correlation and covariance matrices are always Gramian.

IMAGE FACTORING: a method of obtaining initial factors; the observed variation is deomposed into (partial) images and anti-images, instead of into common parts and unique parts.

KAISER CRITERION: a criterion of determining the number of factors to extract; suggested by Guttman and popularized by Kaiser; also known as the "eigenvalue greater than one" criterion.

LINEAR COMBINATION: a combination in which variables are combined with only constant weights.

LINEAR SYSTEM: relationship among variables referred to as a whole, in which all the relationships are linear; factor analysis model in which all of the variables are assumed to be linear functions of underlying factors.

LEAST-SQUARES SOLUTION: in general, a solution which minimizes the squared deviations between the observed values and predicted values; a method of extracting initial factors, whose variants include principal axis factoring with iterated communalities and Minres.

MAXIMUM LIKELIHOOD SOLUTION: in general, a method of statistical estimation which seeks to identify the population parameters with a maximum likelihood of generating the observed sample distribution; a method of obtaining the initial factor solution; its variants include canonical factoring (RAO) and a method that maximizes the determinant of the residual partial correlation matrix.

MONTE CARLO EXPERIMENT: a strategy whereby various sample properties based on complex statistical models are simulated.

OBLIMAX: a criterion for obtaining an oblique rotation: it is equivalent to the quartimax criterion in orthogonal rotation.

OBLIMIN: a general criterion for obtaining an oblique rotation which tries to simplify the pattern matrix by way of reference axes; its variants include bi-quartimin, covarimin, and quartimin.

OBLIQUE FACTORS: factors that are correlated with each other; factors obtained through oblique rotation.

OBLIQUE ROTATION: the operation through which a simple structure is sought; factors are rotated without imposing the orthogonality condition and resulting terminal factors are in general correlated with each other.

ORTHOGONAL FACTORS: factors that are not correlated with each other; factors obtained through orthogonal rotation.

ORTHOGONAL ROTATION: the operation through which a simple structure is sought under the restriction that factors be orthogonal (or uncorrelated); factors obtained through this rotation are by definition uncorrelated.

PRINCIPAL AXIS FACTORING: a method of initial factoring in which the adjusted correlation matrix is decomposed hierarchically; a principal axis factor analysis with iterated communalities leads to a least-squares solution of initial factoring.

PRINCIPAL COMPONENTS: linear combinations of observed variables, possessing properties such as being orthogonal to each other, and the first principal component representing the largest amount of variance in the data, the second representing the second largest and so on; often considered variants of common factors, but more accurately they are contrasted with common factors which are hypothetical.

POSTULATE OF FACTORIAL CAUSATION: the assumption that the observed variables are linear combinations of underlying factors, and that the covariation between observed variables is solely due to their common sharing of one or more of the common factors.

POSTULATE OF PARSIMONY: this stipulates that, given two or more equally compatible models for the given data, the simpler model is believed to be true; in factor analysis, only the model involving the minimum number of common factors is considered appropriate.

QUARTIMAX: a criterion for obtaining an orthogonal rotation; the emphasis is on simplifying the rows of the factor pattern matrix.

QUARTIMIN: a criterion for obtaining an oblique rotation; the oblique counterpart of the quartimax rotation; requires the introduction of reference axes.

RANK OF A MATRIX: the number of linearly independent columns or rows of a matrix; the order of the largest square submatrix whose determinant is not zero.

REFERENCE AXES: these refer to axes that are orthogonal to the primary factors; they are introduced to simplify oblique rotation.

SCREE-TEST: a rule-of-thumb criterion for determining the number of significant factors to retain; it is based on the graph of roots (eigenvalues); claimed to be appropriate in handling disturbances due to minor (unarticulated) factors.

SIMPLE STRUCTURE: a special term referring to a factor structure with certain simple properties; some of these properties include that a variable has factor loadings on as few common factors as possible, and that each common factor has significant loadings on some variables and no loadings on others.

SPECIFIC COMPONENT: the part of the variance of an observed variable that is due to a factor which is specific to a given variable; used to designate the part of the unique component that is not due to random errors.

TARGET MATRIX: a matrix of coefficients used as a target in rotation; an initial factor solution may be rotated in such a way that the resulting factor loadings resemble the target matrix maximally.

VARIANCE: a measure of dispersion of a variable; defined as the sum of squared deviations from the mean divided by the number of cases or entities.

VARIATION: a measure of dispersion in a variable; loosely used as a general term for describing any type of dispersion around some central value; sum of squared deviations from the mean.

VARIMAX: a method of orthogonal rotation which simplifies the factor structure by maximizing the variance of a column of the pattern matrix.

UNIQUE COMPONENT: the part of the observed variance unaccounted for by the common factors; the proportion that is unique to each variable; it is often further decomposed into specific and error components.

UNIQUE FACTOR: the factor which is believed to affect only a single observed variable; often stands for all the independent factors (including the error component) that are unique to a variable.

ABOUT THE AUTHORS

JAE-ON KIM is Professor of Sociology and the director of the Center for Asian and Pacific Studies at the University of Iowa. He received his Ph.D. from the University of California, Berkeley. He specializes in political sociology, social inequality, quantitative methods, and East Asian societies. He has published articles in such journals as American Journal of Sociology, American Political Science Review, American Sociological Review, *and* Social Forces, *and his books include* Equality and Political Participation: A Seven Nation Comparison *(1978), coauthored with Verba and Nie. His current projects are: (1) a comparative study of values of the three East Asian Societies—China, Japan, and Korea; (2) a study of natural experiments in party formation and electoral rules; (3) a joint project to establish general social survey for East Asian Societies; (4) a monograph on sensitivity analysis that deals with problems of imperfect data and incomplete theories in social science research.*

CHARLES W. MUELLER, Professor of Sociology at the University of Iowa, received his undergraduate education at Iowa State University and his Ph.D. from the University of Wisconsin, Madison. He has published articles on social stratification and quantitative methods in such journals as American Sociological Review, Sociological Methods and Research, *and* Work and Occupations. *He is currently involved in research on organizational turnover and employee commitment and satisfaction.*

Quantitative Applications in the Social Sciences

A SAGE UNIVERSITY PAPERS SERIES

$9.95 each

SAGE PUBLICATIONS, INC.
P.O. BOX 5084
THOUSAND OAKS, CALIFORNIA 91359-9924

Place
Stamp
here